BLONDIE'S

Soups • Salads • Sandwiches

COOK BOOK

BLONDIE'S®
COOK BOOK

Soups • Salads • Sandwiches

Chic Young's Classic Cook Book
with New Comic Art Selections
by His Son Dean Young

Gramercy Books
New York • Avenel

This 1996 edition is published by Gramercy Books,
a division of Random House Value Publishing, Inc.,
40 Engelhard Avenue, Avenel, New Jersey 07001,
by arrangement with King Features Syndicate, Inc.

Gramercy Books and colophon are trademarks of
Random House Value Publishing, Inc.

Random House
New York • Toronto • London • Sydney • Auckland
http://www.randomhouse.com/

Printed and bound in the United States of America

*A CIP catalog record for this book is available from the
Library of Congress.*

Blondie's Cook Book / by Chic Young and Dean Young
ISBN 0-517-18087-1

8 7 6 5 4 3 2 1

Editor's Note. Blondie's Cook Book by Chic Young was originally
published in 1947; new illustrations have been added by Dean
Young especially for this edition. The nostalgic recipes in this
book reflect Blondie's and Dagwood's tastes and in no way are
meant to suggest abandoning a healthful and nutritious diet.

CONTENTS

SANDWICHES

Almond	43
Anchovy	13
Apple	9
Baked Bean	11–12
Baking-Powder Biscuit	12
Banana	11
Beef	10
Beef-Heart	10
Beef-Loaf	10
Brown-Bread Cheese	12–13
Cheese Canapés	31
Cheese and Caviar	14
Cheese and Jelly	14
Cheese and Onion	40
Cheese and Peanut Butter	15
Cheese and Pickle	16
Chestnut	31
Chicken and Cranberry	35
Chicken and Ham	35
Chicken and Pimiento	33

SANDWICHES (continued)

Chicken Liver and Bacon	33
Chocolate	37
Club	17
Crab Meat	18
Cucumber and Lettuce	29
Curried Egg and Oyster	26
Daisy	31
Date and Nut	21–22
Deviled Ham	21
Egg and Lettuce	23
Fig	28
Game	30
Ginger and Nut	28
Gingerbread	33–34
Halibut	47
Ham Canapés	34
Ham n' Egg, Cold	32
Ham-Nut	13
Ham-Rusk	34
High School	23

CONTENTS

SANDWICHES (continued)

Horseradish and Tomato 24
Jellied Chicken 24–25
Jellied Tomato 25
Lady-finger 38
Lemon-butter 40
Lenten 39
Lettuce 40–41
Liederkranz Cheese 41
Liver and Chestnut 41
Lobster 44
Maple 45
Marmalade and Nut 43
Marshmallow 47
Mint 45
Mushroom and Lobster 46
Nasturtium 49
New England 50
Nut Canapés 49
Nut and Honey 49
Olive 50
Onion 39
Oyster 38–39
Oyster Canapés 38
Pâté de Foie Gras 48
Pattern 47–48
Peanut 20
Peanut Butter 19
Peanut and Sardine 27
Pepper and Egg 26
Persian 22
Pickle 20
Pineapple 36–37
Pork and Olive 36
Potted Beef 37–38
Raisin 32–33
Rolled 34–35
Salmon 41–42
Sardine Canapés 42
Sardine and Anchovy 42
Sardine-Olive 9
Sardine and Tomato 50–51
Sausage 52

SANDWICHES (continued)

Savory Cream 51
Shad Roe 51
Shrimp 19
Skyscraper Special 8
Spanish 18
Strawberry 22
Sunday Night Canapés 44
Tango 46
Tongue 16
Tongue Canapés 48
Tricolored 16–17
Tutti Frutti 25
Vegetable and Cheese 27

SOUPS

Angelemono 59
Bean 57
Beef Shank Barley 56
Beef and Vegetable
  Chowder 56
Celery 57
Chicken 58
Chicken Broth, Jellied 63
Clam Chowder 58
Cream of Asparagus 58
Cream of Carrot 60
Cream of Chicken and
  Corn 59
Cream of Corn 61
Cream of Mushroom 60
Cream of Spinach 60
Cream of Vegetable 61
Fish Chowder 62
Foundation Soup Stock 55
Kidney Bean and Rice 61
Lentil 63
Minestrone 65
Mock Turtle 65
Mulligatawny 65–66
Mushroom Broth 66–67
Okra 66
Onion 67

CONTENTS

SOUPS (continued)

Onion, with Cheese 68
Oyster 64
Philadelphia Pepper Pot 64
Potato 67
Potato Chowder 67–68
Potato and Corn
Chowder 71
Potato and Onion 68
Pot-Luck 63
Split Pea 69
Tomato 70
Tomato Bisque 71
Tomato Consommé 70
Turnip, Quick 69
Vegetable Thrift 72
Watercress and
Cheese 71–72
Yankee Corn Chowder 72

SALADS

Anchovy and Walnut 125
Artichoke 75–76
Asparagus 76
Asparagus and Ham 76–77
Avocado and Grapefruit 77
Banana and Date 77–78
Beet, Jellied, and Nut 103
Beet and Onion 78
Bermuda 78
Blue Bird 79
Cabbage, in Cabbage
Shell 80
Cabbage and Celery 79–80
Calf's Brain 83
Cantaloupe 82
Carrot 81
Casaba or Honeydew
Melon 82–83
Cauliflower and Beet 81–82
Cheese 83–84
Cheese, Frozen 94

SALADS (continued)

Cherry and Cream
Cheese 84
Chestnut and Celery 84–85
Chicken, No. 1 85–86
Chicken, No. 2 86
Chicken, Jellied, and
Rice 100
Chicory 86–87
Chiffonade 87
Church-supper 92
Cole-Slaw 88
Cordial 127–128
Corn, Nut and Celery 89
Crab-Meat 89–90
Cream Cheese and
Pimiento 87
Cream Cheese and Pine-
apple 88
Dandelion 90
Dandelion and Oyster 91
Egg 91
Egg and Lobster 90
Endive 91–92
Fish, No. 1 92–93
Fish, No. 2 93
Frogs' Legs 93–94
Fruit 94–97
Fruit, Jellied, and
Celery 104
Fruit, à la Russe 97
Fruits Glacé 117–118
Ginger Ale 99
Green Dressing 99–100
Ham, Jellied 104
Herring 98
Horseradish and Celery 100
Hot Slaw 102
Imperial 103
Italian 103–104
Kumquat 105
Lettuce, and Roquefort
Dressing 106–107

CONTENTS

SALADS (continued)

Lobster, No. 1   105
Lobster, No. 2   106
Macaroni   126–127
Macédoine   101
Merry Maze   107
Mint   106
Nut   108
Nut and Prune   107
Okra   108
Olive and Celery   110
Orange and Tomato   109
Oyster   111
Oyster and Egg   109
Park Lane   110
Pea and Pickle   110–111
Pea and Walnut   111
Peach   112–113
Peanut and Celery   112
Pear   114
Pimiento   113
Pineapple and
  Grapefruit   113–114
Potato, No. 1   115
Potato, No. 2   115–116
Potato, No. 3   116
Queen   115
Radish   116–117
Red Kidney Bean   117
Romaine   117
Salad Dressing, Boiled   89
Salmon   121
Salmon and Oyster   118
Saratoga   119
Sardine   119
Scallop   119–120
Shrimp, Celery and Nut   120
Spanish Onion and
  Sardine   120
Spinach   121
Strawberry   122
String-Bean   122–123

SALADS (continued)

Sweetbread   123
Tomato, Frozen   99
Tomato, Stuffed   123
Tomato Jelly   124
Tongue   124–125
Tripe   125
Tropic   75
Tuna Fish   125–126
Turnip   126
Vegetable, Hot   101–102
Vegetable, in Shells   127
Waldorf   128
Watermelon   128–129
Western   129
Yukon   129

PICNIC FARE

Adam and Eve on a
  Raft   134
Cherry Punch, Sweet   140
Chicken Liver
  Spread   134–135
Egg Salad Spread   137
Eggs, Bedeviled   135
Gingerbread   138
Grape Cocktail Deluxe   139
Grape and Tea Rickey   139
Hamburgers, Broiled
  Deviled   136
Hamburger Roll   136
Lemonade, Old Fash-
  ioned   140
Liver Sausage-burgers,
  Grilled   134
Pickles, Dill   137
Po' Boy Sandwich   133–134
Popovers   138
Potato Salad   135
Punch Supreme   139
Sandwich Fillers   133
Slaw, Vegetable   138

SAYS DAGWOOD:

Food is a very interesting subject. Believe it or not, gravity is what limits a sandwich's size. For instance, take a sandwich that gets too high—the top layer always rolls off. That's where practice and experience in building comes in. I always use a good flat matter for the top layer and make sure while I'm building to mix in a good mortar of ketchup with horseradish, mustard and mayonnaise. This makes a firmer foundation and a taller skyscraper possible. You'll be able to do it too after you've given my Special a few tries. Blondie's book is filled with good things to eat. Sandwiches, for instance.

SAYS BLONDIE:

When Dagwood makes a sandwich he needs stacks of bread and a full icebox. However, tasty snacks worthy of the name of sandwich can be made with almost anything—as you'll notice in going through the pages of this book. Sandwiches, that is the kind we have when Dagwood doesn't have a hand in them, are popular with all members of the family on any occasion. And with soup, and salad, they are the "Three S's" with which you can provide a satisfactory meal on short shift. This is a collection of Bumstead favorites. A few of our favorites, such as "hot dog" sandwiches, are omitted because the recipes are too obvious or well known.

IN 1758, the Earl of Sandwich, rebelling against the tyranny of a "no gambling at mealtime" law, ordered that pieces of meat should be laid between two slices of bread and brought to him as he sat at play. Thus was the sandwich born.

But the ultimate in sandwichdom remained for almost two centuries later, when late in the 1930s, the super-sandwich of all time— The Dagwood—was born.

Skyscraper Special (aka The Dagwood)

Slice of buttered bread
Layer of crisp lettuce (or watercress or endive)
Cold, sliced chicken (or ham or veal or pork or potroast or turkey or cold cuts or bacon or sausage or almost anything)
Thin slices of hard boiled egg (or a fried egg)
Layer of American cheese (or cottage or Swiss or cream cheese)
Layer of sliced tomatoes
Sardines (or anchovies or smoked salmon)
Slice of onion
Cold, baked beans
Second layer of lettuce
Second slice of buttered bread

Start building with crisp lettuce, continue with sliced

chicken, egg, cheese, tomato, etc. Additions which may be inserted to taste are: sliced pineapple, chopped or sliced pickle, pickled beets, olives, cucumbers, Russian dressing, ketchup, mayonnaise, horseradish, salt and pepper.

Sardine-Olive Sandwich

Buttered slices bread	Pounded hard-cooked egg-
Chopped olives	yolks
Chopped pimientoes	Shredded lettuce
Pounded sardines	Mayonnaise dressing
Chopped parsley	Salt and pepper to taste

Spread a slice of lightly buttered bread with the olives and a layer of mayonnaise; place another slice of bread on top, buttered side up, spread with pounded sardines and mayonnaise; place another slice of bread on top, buttered side up, spread with pounded sardines and mayonnaise; place another slice of bread on top, buttered side up, spread with pimientoes and mayonnaise; put another slice of bread on top, buttered side up, spread with egg-yolks and mayonnaise; again another slice, buttered side up, spread with lettuce mixed with mayonnaise, and top with a slice of bread; place under a weight. Decorate with chopped parsley and serve cut in slices.

Apple Sandwiches

4 apples	2 ozs. (½ cup) grated
2 tablespoonfuls lemon-	cheese
juice	Brown bread
1 gill (½ cup) stiff mayon-	White bread
naise dressing	

Grate the apples and mix them at once with the lemon-juice; add the mayonnaise and the grated cheese, and serve between a slice of white bread and a slice of brown bread.

Another Method.—Chop two peeled apples, add one cupful of stoned and chopped raisins, one cupful of chopped pecan-nut meats, the strained juice of a small lemon, and two teaspoonfuls of sugar. Mix well and spread between thin slices of buttered bread.

Beef Sandwiches

Thinly cut cooked beef	Salt and pepper to taste
Curry butter	Parsley or watercress
Skinned, sliced tomatoes	Bread

To make the curry butter: Beat one-half cupful of sweet butter to a cream, add a tablespoonful of curry powder, one-half teaspoonful of lemon-juice, and salt to taste.

Cut some slices of bread and spread with curry butter, cover with the beef, add some slices of tomato, seasoned with salt and pepper, cover with another piece of bread spread with curry butter, and press together. Serve garnished with parsley or watercress.

Beef-Heart Sandwiches

1 cooked beef heart	1 teaspoonful mustard
½ pint (1 cup) stock or water	½ teaspoonful salt
	¼ teaspoonful pepper
1 teaspoonful meat extract	½ tablespoonful chopped parsley
½ oz. (1 tablespoonful) butter	Hot toast

Chop the heart, then place it in a pan with the butter, water, parsley, extract, and seasonings. When hot and thoroughly mixed, serve between thin slices of hot buttered toast.

Beef-Loaf Sandwiches

Beef loaf	Worcestershire sauce
Buttered bread	Parsley or watercress

Put a thin slice of a cooked beef loaf between thin slices of buttered bread. Press the slices together and cut into triangles. Serve decorated with watercress or parsley.

If liked, a few drops of Worcestershire sauce may be sprinkled over the slices of beef loaf.

Banana Sandwiches

2 bananas
½ pint (1 cup) chopped
   English walnut meats
Mayonnaise dressing

Lettuce leaves
¼ teaspoonful sugar
Bread
Parsley

Mash the bananas, stir in the nuts and sugar. Spread mayonnaise and then the banana filling on thin slices of bread. Place lettuce leaves between the slices, and serve garnished with parsley.

Baked Bean Sandwiches

Baked beans
Grated cheese
Butter
Chopped parsley

Salt and pepper
Lemon-juice
Buttered bread

Rub a quantity of baked beans through a sieve, and to every cupful of the paste add one tablespoonful of grated cheese, one teaspoonful of chopped parsley, one teaspoonful of lemon-juice, one tablespoonful of melted butter, and salt and pepper to taste. Spread this paste thickly between slices of buttered brown or white bread.

Or cut bread in one-fourth inch slices, spread one-half with the mixture, and cut with a round cutter having the same diameter as a doughnut cutter. Cut the remaining pieces with a doughnut cutter, and place these over the spread pieces.

Baking-Powder Biscuit Sandwiches

Baking-powder biscuits
½ pint (1 cup) chopped
  cooked chicken
3 hard-cooked eggs
4 tablespoonfuls grated
  cheese

½ teaspoonful mustard
Salt and pepper to taste
2 tablespoonfuls tarragon
  vinegar
Salad oil
Butter or oleo

Cut the baking-powder biscuits in three layers and butter them. Pound the chicken with the eggs, add the cheese, seasonings, vinegar, and sufficient oil to moisten. Rub through a wire sieve and spread on the layers; put the slices together and serve on a folded napkin.

Brown-Bread Cheese Sandwiches

Brown bread
Chopped English walnut
  meats
Chopped celery or cucum-
  ber
½ lb. cheese
2 ozs. (4 tablespoonfuls)
  sweet butter

4 tablespoonfuls cream
Salt and pepper
1 teaspoonful vinegar
Lettuce leaves or water-
  cress
Paprika

Rub the cheese through a sieve, put it into a basin with the butter, cream, vinegar, salt and pepper to taste, and mix until smooth. Cut some brown bread into thin slices and spread it about one-fourth of an inch thick with the cheese mixture. Sprinkle this with a little paprika, and on it put a sprinkling of finely chopped walnut meats, and some very finely chopped celery or cucumber. Cover this with another slice of bread that has also some of the cheese cream spread on it, and cut out the sandwiches with a plain or fancy cutter.

Garnish each sandwich with a little of the cheese cream, using a bag with a small star tube for the purpose. Serve on a dish on a fancy paper, garnished with tiny lettuce leaves or watercress.

Ham-Nut Sandwiches

4 slices cold boiled ham
4 skinned and sliced to-
   matoes
¼ pint (½ cup) chopped
   English walnut meats

Cream cheese
Mayonnaise dressing
Lettuce leaves
Green onions
8 slices buttered bread

Trim the crusts from the slices of bread, and on four slices place a slice of boiled ham and spread over with mayonnaise dressing. Over these put the remaining slices of bread, buttered sides up, and on these spread the cheese; then place thinly sliced tomatoes on the top. Cover generously with mayonnaise dressing, sprinkle over with the nuts, and serve on crisp lettuce leaves garnished with the green onions.

Anchovy Sandwiches

12 anchovies
4 tablespoonfuls anchovy
   paste
½ lb. (1 cup) sweet butter

6 tablespoonfuls chopped
   parsley
1 teaspoonful chopped
   chives
Buttered brown bread

Cream one-half of the butter, add the parsley, chives, mix well, and spread one-fourth of an inch thick on one piece of buttered brown bread. Cream the remaining butter, add the anchovy paste, the anchovies skinned and pounded to a paste, mix well, then spread one-fourth of an inch thick on buttered brown bread, place on the top of the other, and cut into fancy shapes.

A sandwich of anchovy paste and whipped cream has an appeal when properly prepared.

Cheese and Caviar Sandwiches

Buttered bread   Caviar
Cream cheese   Black pepper
Cream

Butter some thin slices of white bread; soften some cream
cheese with cream until it will spread easily; spread this on the
buttered bread, and on this spread a little caviar. Spread both
sides of the sandwich with butter and cheese, but only one side
with caviar. Season with pepper. Trim the crusts from the
slices and cut them into dainty shapes with cutters.

Another Caviar Sandwich.—Mix one-half can of caviar with
one teaspoonful of onion-juice and one teaspoonful of lemon-
juice. Spread between thin rounds of buttered bread or
crackers.

Or, add chopped nut meats or chopped olives to caviar, mix
with a little wine, and use as a filling for sandwiches.

The caviar referred to in this book is not the expensive im-
ported sturgeon caviar, but the moderately-priced American,
whitefish caviar.

Cheese and Jelly Sandwiches

Cream cheese   Blanched and chopped
Currant jelly   pistachio nuts
                              Buttered bread

Stamp out thin slices of white bread with a cutter. Butter
and spread half of these with cream cheese and currant jelly
mixed to a pink cream. On the top place a second round of
bread buttered and sprinkled with the chopped nuts.

To add some variety, chop some canned pineapple fine
and drain off the juice. Spread bread thinly with cream cheese,
sprinkle with the chopped pineapple, and press together. Cut
in thin, slender strips.

An additional sandwich filling may be made by mixing
orange marmalade, finely chopped pecan-nut meats, and cream
cheese. Spread this mixture between slices of buttered whole-
wheat bread and cut in long narrow strips.

Cheese and Peanut Butter Sandwiches

½ pint (1 cup) peanut butter
½ pint (1 cup) cream cheese
Brown bread
Salt and pepper to taste
½ tablespoonful orange-juice
1 oz. (2 tablespoonfuls) butter or oleo

Cream the butter, add the peanut butter, cheese, and seasonings, and spread on small rounds of thinly cut brown bread. Serve with crisp celery.

Another Method.—Chop tender and crisp radishes fine; chill on the ice; then mix with them grated American cheese and peanut butter. Spread between small rounds of buttered bread.

Or mix peeled and chopped cucumbers with grated Parmesan cheese and a little red pepper, and spread between thin slices of either white or brown bread spread with peanut butter. Cut into triangles.

The best peanut butter is made from a mixture of Virginia and Spanish types of nuts. A straight Virginia butter lacks smoothness and straight Spanish lacks flavor and is too oily.

Cheese and Pickle Sandwiches

1 lb. moist cheese	Salt and paprika to taste
½ pint (1 cup) sour pickles	Brown or white bread
1 lb. (2 cups) butter	

Put the cheese and pickles through a food-chopper and season to taste with salt and paprika. Cream the butter and combine gradually with the cheese mixture. Chill and spread evenly on thin slices of bread and press together.

Tongue Sandwiches

½ pint (1 cup) chopped cooked tongue	¼ teaspoonful paprika
1 teaspoonful mustard	1 hard-cooked egg-yolk
1 teaspoonful butter	½ lemon
	Pinch grated nutmeg

Mix the tongue with the yolk of egg, add the butter, strained lemon-juice, and the seasonings. Spread between thin slices of buttered bread and cut in triangles.

Another Method.—Put one-half pound each of cooked tongue and boiled ham through a food-chopper, add salt, pepper, and grated nutmeg to taste. Stir in one-half cupful of melted butter, one tablespoonful of chopped olives, and a small bottle of pickles chopped fine. Cut the bread as thin as possible. Spread it with some of the meat mixture, cover with a layer of washed and drained cress, and place another slice of the bread on the top. Cut into small sandwiches.

Tricolored Sandwiches

6 slices bread	Deviled ham
Potted egg	Aspic jelly
Vegetable-dyed butter	Butter or margarine

Butter the slices of bread and make three sandwiches, one with potted egg, one with the deviled ham, and the other with the green butter. Now put a little softened butter on them and stick all three sandwiches together, press them lightly, trim off the crusts, and cut them into six pieces; dip each one into liquid aspic jelly that is just about to set, and put them in a cool place or in a refrigerator until required.

To make the potted egg: Hard-cook three eggs, allow them to get cold, pass the yolks through a sieve, beat them with a tablespoonful of butter, season to taste with salt and paprika.

Club Sandwiches

Breast cold roast turkey or
    chicken
Broiled bacon or ham
Crisp white lettuce leaf
Dill pickles or tomato
Mayonnaise dressing
Toasted sliced white bread
Parsley
Butter or margarine

Trim crust from large square slices of bread and toast a delicate brown; then butter them. Insert a layer of bacon, one of thinly sliced dill pickle or tomato, and one of cold fowl. Cover with a lettuce leaf spread with mayonnaise, add top slice of toast, trim neatly, and cut diagonally into triangles. Garnish with parsley and serve immediately on hot plates.

These sandwiches, to be at their best, should be made and served in the shortest possible time.

In a club sandwich, which in itself is a very fair luncheon, the chicken should be thin, the bacon very crisp, the lettuce fresh, and the mayonnaise and butter plentiful.

To make a cold club sandwich use moderately thin cut bread in place of the toast, and substitute cold sliced ham for the crisped bacon. The chicken, lettuce, and dressing remain the same.

Crab Meat Sandwiches

1 oz. (2 tablespoonfuls) butter	⅛ teaspoonful baking soda
2 tablespoonfuls chopped pimientoes	½ lb. (2 cups) diced cheese
½ oz. (2 tablespoonfuls) flour	1 egg
1 gill (½ cup) cream	½ pint (1 cup) cooked crab meat
1½ gills (¾ cup) stewed tomatoes	1 teaspoonful salt
	½ teaspoonful pepper
	½ teaspoonful mustard

Melt the butter, add pimientoes, and cook for three minutes, stirring constantly. Add flour and stir until blended; then stir in the cream and strained tomatoes, to which has been added the soda. Now add the cheese, and when melted, the egg slightly beaten, seasonings, and crab meat. When heated, spread between slices of buttered toasted bread. Cut into desired shapes and serve.

Chopped green pepper may be substituted for the pimiento, and canned tuna fish or canned crab meat for the cooked crab meat.

Spanish Sandwiches

3 pimientoes	1 tablespoonful flour
¼ lb. cheese	1 tablespoonful sugar
2 hard-cooked eggs	3 tablespoonfuls vinegar
1 small onion	1 teaspoonful salt
1 beaten egg	⅛ teaspoonful red pepper
1 tablespoonful butter	Lettuce leaves

Put the pimientoes, hard-cooked eggs, and cheese through a food-chopper, add the onion, chopped, and mix well.

Put the raw egg into the upper pan of a double boiler, stir in the sugar and flour, add the butter, salt, red pepper, and vinegar, and cook over hot water until a paste is formed. Mix with the other ingredients and set aside to cool.

Serve on slices of buttered bread with lettuce leaves between.

Shrimp Sandwiches

4 tablespoonfuls of picked shrimps	1½ teaspoonfuls anchovy paste
3 tablespoonfuls whipped cream	Buttered rolls
	Paprika to taste

Chop the shrimps, mix them with the anchovy paste, paprika, and whipped cream. Spread this mixture between buttered rolls, and serve garnished with the parsley.

Peanut Butter Sandwiches

8 tablespoonfuls peanut butter	¼ lb. (1 cup) seeded raisins, chopped
¼ lb. (1 cup) chopped pecan nut meats	4 tablespoonfuls lemon-juice
Cream	Sugar

Beat the peanut butter with the lemon-juice, add the nuts and raisins, sugar to taste, and enough cream to moisten. Mix well and spread between buttered bread or crackers.

Peanut Sandwiches

½ pint (1 cup) shelled and chopped peanuts	½ lemon
⅓ cupful vinegar	1½ gills (¾ cup) sour cream
2 ozs. (¼ cup) sugar	Lettuce leaves
¼ teaspoonful salt	Buttered bread
⅛ teaspoonful pepper	1 egg

Put the vinegar into a small saucepan and bring to boiling-point. Beat up the egg and mix it with the sour cream, add the sugar, salt, and pepper, and put all into the hot vinegar. Stir until it boils, then remove from the fire and allow to cool before pouring it over the peanuts. Add enough strained lemon-juice to make the mixture tart. Spread between slices of buttered bread with a crisp lettuce leaf between.

Another Method—Secure fresh roasted peanuts or buy them shelled, by the pound. Remove the inner hull and put them in the oven to brown nicely. Turn them out on a board and crush fine with a rolling-pin. Place them in a bowl and mix thoroughly with mayonnaise dressing. The cooked mayonnaise, without oil, makes a delicious combination. Spread between slices of thin buttered bread and cut into cutlet shapes.

If liked, cream cheese may be added and the mixture spread between crackers.

Pickle Sandwiches

4 chopped pickles	1 tablespoonful grated fresh horseradish
3 tablespoonfuls whipped cream	8 tablespoonfuls mayonnaise or boiled dressing
Chopped cooked beef	Buttered bread

Mix together the cream, mayonnaise, or boiled dressing, horseradish, and pickles. Spread buttered bread with this mixture, then with a thin layer of beef, and cover with more dressing and bread. Cut into shapes.

Deviled Ham Sandwiches

Buttered bread or crackers	½ pint (1 cup) milk
Deviled ham	Paprika to taste
2 eggs	Hot melted butter

Butter thin slices of bread or crackers and upon half of the buttered pieces spread some deviled ham. Finish with the other slices of buttered bread and cut in halves.

Beat up the eggs, add the milk and paprika to taste. Soak the sandwiches in this mixture until they are saturated, then cook in hot butter until browned, first on one side and then on the other. Serve hot.

Grated cheese may be used in place of the deviled ham.

Another Method.—Beat the yolks of three eggs in a small saucepan, add one tablespoonful of flour mixed with one teaspoonful of mustard, one teaspoonful of salt, three tablespoonfuls of sugar; mix well, then add one teacupful of vinegar, and stir and cook until it boils. Cool and mix with a can of deviled ham and spread on crackers.

Date and Nut Sandwiches

6 ozs. (1½ cups) nut meats	6 ozs. (1½ cups) stoned dates

Butter   Thick cream
Lemon-juice   Whole-wheat bread

Put the nuts and dates through a food-chopper, add lemon-juice to taste, and enough cream to make it of a consistency to spread. Butter a thin slice of bread, then spread with the filling, and finish with an unbuttered slice. Cut into fingers.

Strawberry Sandwiches

10 or 12 strawberries   1 teaspoonful strawberry
¼ lb. (½ cup) butter   extract
6½ ozs. (1 cup) confec-   Fresh bread
tioners' sugar

Cream the butter until soft; add the sugar, the strawberries mashed, and strawberry extract. Mix all well together and chill on ice. Cut the crusts from fresh bread slices, spread with the mixture, and wrap in a cloth for several hours. The bread can be rolled up after being spread with the mixture, or it can be cut into fancy shapes.

Another Method.—Cut some thin slices of bread. Spread one-half with whipped cream and sprinkle over with sugar. Slightly butter the remaining slices, and cover with sliced strawberries. Press the two slices together.

Persian Sandwiches

½ lb. stoned dates   ½ lb. preserved cherries
½ lb. figs   1 lemon
½ lb. English walnut   1 teaspoonful almond ex-
meats   tract
½ lb. peanut butter   Unsweetened crackers

Put the figs, dates, and cherries through a food-chopper. Cut the nut meats into small pieces and add them, with the peanut butter, almond extract, and enough strained lemon-juice to make a paste soft enough to mold into flat wafers one-fourth of an inch thick.

Serve between saltines or any unsweetened cracker.

If liked, a little chopped canned pineapple may be added to the above.

Egg and Lettuce Sandwiches

4 hard-cooked eggs	2 tablespoonfuls chopped
Crisp lettuce leaves	celery
Mayonnaise dressing	4 drops onion-juice

Chop the eggs, add the celery, onion-juice, and enough mayonnaise dressing to make the mixture spread nicely, and place with a lettuce leaf between buttered bread.

High School Sandwiches

Chopped English walnut	¼ lb. (½ cup) sugar
meats	½ teaspoonful salt
Buttered bread	1 tablespoonful flour
Crisp lettuce leaves	3 tablespoonfuls vinegar
1 lemon	½ oz. (1 tablespoonful)
4 egg-yolks	butter
	½ pint (1 cup) water

Strain the juice of lemon into a saucepan; add yolks of eggs mixed with the sugar, salt, flour, vinegar, butter, and water. Stir and cook until thick, then cool and add as many walnut meats as desired. Spread this dressing over a crisp lettuce leaf and place between thin slices of buttered bread.

The whites of eggs may be used for cake or meringue.

Horseradish and Tomato Sandwiches

¼ pint (½ cup) grated horseradish	Salt
	White bread
Skinned, sliced tomatoes	Butter
¼ pint (½ cup) mayonnaise dressing	Parsley

Sprinkle the tomato slices with salt. Spread thin slices of buttered bread with the horseradish and the mayonnaise mixed together; put the slices of tomato between, cut into fancy shapes, and serve garnished with parsley.

Jellied Chicken Sandwiches

1 boiled chicken	½ pint (1 cup) cream
2 stalks celery	½ tablespoonful lemon-juice
1 teaspoonful grated onion	Salt, pepper, and paprika to taste
2 tablespoonfuls powdered gelatine	Buttered brown or white bread
1 gill (¼ cup) hot water	

Put the meat of the chicken and celery through a food-chopper, then add the onion, seasonings, cream, and the gelatine dissolved in the water. Turn into a wet, shallow dish and set on ice for two hours. Cut into thin slices and place between buttered slices of brown or white bread. If liked, a little grated horseradish may be added.

Jellied Tomato Sandwiches

1 can tomatoes	Tabasco sauce to taste
1 oz. (3 tablespoonfuls) powdered gelatine	2 chopped pimientoes (canned red peppers)
2 tablespoonfuls vinegar	2 tablespoonsful chopped nut meats
1 teaspoonful sugar	
½ teaspoonful salt	2 tablespoonfuls chopped celery
¼ teaspoonful pepper	
½ teaspoonful celery salt	Lettuce leaves
1 teaspoonful Worcestershire sauce	Mayonnaise dressing
	Buttered bread

Boil and strain the tomatoes, add the gelatine and seasonings. When cool, add pimientoes, nut meats, and celery. Spread when cold on buttered slices of bread, add a lettuce leaf dipped in mayonnaise dressing, and top with a slice of buttered bread. Cut into squares and serve on a sandwich tray.

Tutti Frutti Sandwiches

½ pint (1 cup) seeded raisins	1 lb. figs
½ pint (1 cup) stoned dates	Juice ½ lemon
	1 teaspoonful almond extract
½ pint (1 cup) hot water	Whipped cream
3 ozs. (¾ cup) chopped nut meats	Angelica, candied violets
	Sweet wafers

Chop the figs, raisins, and dates, put them into a saucepan with the water, and cook slowly until thick. Take from the fire, add the nuts, the strained lemon-juice, and the almond extract. Cool and spread between wafers and decorate the top with whipped cream, candied violets, and strips of angelica.

Pepper and Egg Sandwiches

6 green bell peppers
½ pint (1 cup) English
   walnut meats
1 lettuce heart

½ pint (1 cup) chopped
   cooked bacon
Mayonnaise dressing
2 hard-cooked eggs

Chop the peppers, nuts, lettuce, and eggs; add the bacon and enough mayonnaise to bind the ingredients together. Spread this mixture on squares of bread, and cover with squares which have been spread with mayonnaise dressing. These sandwiches are delicious served with salad.

Curried Egg and Oyster Sandwiches

½ pint (1 cup) chopped
   hard-cooked eggs
½ pint (1 cup) cooked
   oysters

Curry powder to taste
1 teaspoonful onion-juice
Cream
Buttered bread

Chop the slightly cooked oysters with the eggs, add seasonings to taste, and moisten with cream. Spread between thin squares of buttered bread. Of course, Curry powder is tastiest when "cooked in." Try cooking it in the oysters.

Vegetable and Cheese Sandwiches

1 Liederkranz cheese	Lettuce leaves
Radishes	Boiled dressing
Young onions	Bread

Cut the green tops from some young onions and some radishes and slice both very thinly lengthwise. Let them lie with some crisp lettuce leaves for one hour in ice water. Then drain and dry. Dip a leaf of lettuce into boiled dressing, and lay it on a slice of bread; over this place a layer of cheese, then a layer of radish, a layer of onions, some more cheese, then another leaf of lettuce dipped in dressing, and a slice of bread.

Peanut and Sardine Sandwiches

½ pint (1 cup) shelled	Mayonnaise or boiled
peanuts	dressing
2 cans sardines	Buttered rye bread

Put the peanuts through a food-chopper and mix them thoroughly with the sardines, pounded to a paste; add sufficient dressing to hold together, and spread between slices of rye bread.

Cut in triangles and serve.

Fig Sandwiches

½ lb. (2 cups) chopped   ¼ lb. (½ cup) sugar
    figs   ¼ lb. (½ cup) butter
1 gill (½ cup) water   Bread

Put the figs through a food-chopper, add the sugar and water, and cook until thick. Cool, add the butter, and mix well. Spread between thin slices of bread. If liked, one-half cupful of chopped nut meats may be added.

Another Method.—Put three-fourths cupful of water into a saucepan with one and one-half cupfuls of light brown sugar, and one teaspoonful of butter, and boil to a thick syrup; then take from the fire and add one-half pound of chopped figs, one-half pound of chopped cocoanut, and one-half cupful of chopped English walnut meats.

Chill, and use with bread or crackers.

Or soak eight figs in hot water for two minutes, then drain and dry them, slice them in halves lengthwise, fill with chopped English walnut meats, and serve between crackers.

Ginger and Nut Sandwiches

½ pint (1 cup) chopped   ¼ pint (½ cup) chopped
    preserved ginger   candied orange-peel
½ pint (1 cup) chopped   Vinegar
    nut meats   Buttered bread

Mix the ginger, nuts, and peel together; add a few drops of vinegar and enough of the preserved ginger syrup to bind the mixture. Spread between thin slices of buttered whole-wheat bread. Cut into fancy shapes and serve at afternoon tea.

Another Method.—Put two cupfuls of preserved ginger through a food-chopper with one-half cupful of preserved cherries; add the strained juice of one orange and two table-spoonfuls of whipped cream; spread between very thin slices of buttered bread, cut in circles or squares, decorate with halves of cherries, and serve with tea or chocolate.

Cucumber and Lettuce Sandwiches

½ pint (1 cup) boiled dressing

1 gill (½ cup) whipped cream

Crisp lettuce leaves

Peeled and sliced cucumbers

Vinegar and onion-juice to taste

Salt, pepper, and paprika to taste

Buttered whole-wheat bread

Ground nut meats

Mix the whipped cream with the boiled dressing and spread on slices of whole-wheat bread. Sprinkle over with a layer of ground nut meats, and on one slice lay two or three thinly sliced pieces of cucumber seasoned with vinegar, onion-juice, salt, pepper, and paprika. On the other slice of the sandwich place one or two lettuce leaves and press the slices lightly together.

The nuts may be omitted.

Another Method.—Delicious sandwiches may be made by dipping thin slices of cucumber in well-seasoned French dressing or mayonnaise, and placing, with a sprinkling of finely chopped fresh mint, between thin slices of white bread spread with sweet butter. Cut into star shapes.

Game Sandwiches

Cold cooked game
2 ozs. (4 tablespoonfuls)
   butter
2 tablespoonfuls whipped
   cream

Salt, pepper, and paprika
   to taste
Watercress or parsley
3 hard-cooked egg-yolks
Buttered bread

Take away all skin, bone, and gristle from cold cooked game and chop it, making one cupful. Put this with the egg-yolks, butter, and seasonings into a basin and pound well; then add the cream and mix thoroughly. Spread between slices of buttered bread, press lightly together, cut into rounds or any shape desired. Garnish with watercress or sprigs of parsley.

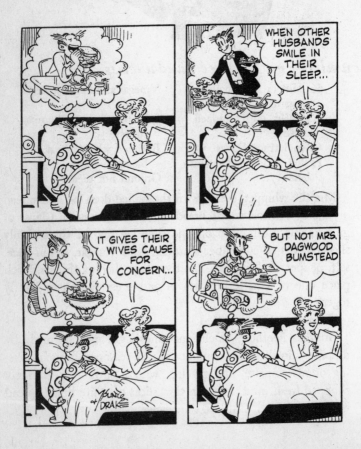

Cheese Canapés

¼ lb. cheese	Salt and red pepper
8 rounds bread	1 teaspoonful mild mus-
1 oz. (2 tablespoonfuls)	tard
butter	2 teaspoonfuls sherry

Cut rounds of stale or toasted bread; fry the rounds a golden color in hot fat. Cut the cheese into small pieces and pound it to a paste with the butter; then add the seasonings and the sherry wine. When mixed, spread on the croûtes of bread; place in the oven until hot through and serve immediately.

Daisy Sandwiches

Bread	Butter
Grated cheese	Lettuce leaves
Eggs	Salt and pepper to taste

Allow one slice of light bread, three-fourths of an inch thick, and an egg to each person. Cut the bread in rounds, spread with butter, and brown lightly. Cool and spread with grated cheese. Beat up the whites of the eggs, season with salt, pile them on the top of the rounds, make a depression in the top of each white, and fill with the unbroken yolks of eggs. Sprinkle with pepper and bake in a hot oven until the whites are slightly browned. Serve on lettuce leaves.

Chestnut Sandwiches

½ pint (1 cup) boiled chestnuts	Salt and pepper to taste
	1 teaspoonful lemon-juice
½ oz. (1 tablespoonful)	1 gill (½ cup) cream
butter	Buttered bread or cake

Put the chestnuts through a food-chopper. Melt the butter in a saucepan, add the chestnuts, stir for a minute, then add the cream and seasonings and cook until slightly browned. Cool and use between thin pieces of buttered bread or cake.

Cold Ham n' Egg Sandwiches

¼ lb. (1 cup) cooked
    ham
2 sweet pickles
½ can pimientoes

Boiled dressing
1 teaspoonful chopped
    parsley
2 hard-cooked eggs

Put the ham, pickles, eggs, and pimientoes through a food-chopper; add the parsley and mix with sufficient dressing to moisten. Spread between thin slices of buttered bread and cut into triangles.

Raisin Sandwiches

¼ lb. (1 cup) seeded
    raisins
¼ lb. chopped nuts
½ tablespoonful lemon-
    juice

2 ozs. (4 tablespoonfuls)
    sweet butter
Toasted crackers or brown
    bread
A few boiled raisins

Wash, dry, and chop the raisins, add the nut meats, lemon-juice, and butter; mix to a paste and spread between toasted crackers or thin slices of brown bread. Decorate with boiled raisins.

Or mix equal quantities of chopped raisins and chopped pecan nut meats, add four tablespoonfuls of boiled or mayonnaise dressing and one teaspoonful of lemon-juice; when smooth, spread between slices of buttered bread. Cut in crescents or squares.

Chicken Liver and Bacon Sandwiches

Chicken livers	Crisped bacon
Salt	Buttered bread
Pepper	Parsley

Cook and cool the required amount of chicken-livers; mash them to a paste, season to taste with salt and pepper, and spread over thin slices of buttered bread. Cover with shreds of crisped bacon and place other slices of bread on the top. Cut into rounds, ovals, triangles, or fingers, and serve garnished with parsley.

Chicken and Pimiento Sandwiches

1 boiled chicken	3 tablespoonfuls vinegar
1 can pimientoes	1 tablespoonful Worcestershire sauce
3 small pickles	
6 hard-cooked eggs	Buttered bread

Drain the pimientoes and put them through a food-chopper with the meat of the chicken, pickles, and eggs. Moisten with the oil from the pimientoes, then add the vinegar and sauce. Mix and spread on thinly sliced buttered bread and cut in diamond-shaped pieces. Sufficient for four dozen sandwiches.

Gingerbread Sandwiches

Gingerbread	Honey
Butter	

Cut very thin slices from a flat cake of gingerbread. Butter each slice and spread with honey alternately; place two together, spread side uppermost, and then cover with a plain slice.

Press these triple sandwiches gently together, cut in halves or quarters, and serve for afternoon tea.

Ham Canapés

¼ lb. (1 cup) chopped cooked ham	1 oz. (¼ cup) grated Parmesan cheese
1 gill (½ cup) cream	Red pepper to taste
Chutney	Bread

Cut some bread in rounds and fry these to a golden color in hot fat. Pound the ham and mix it with the cream; then spread thickly on the croûtes of bread; over that put a layer of chutney, then a layer of cheese which has been seasoned with a little red pepper. Place in the oven to brown the cheese and serve at once.

Ham-Rusk Sandwiches

Rusks	1 tablespoonful chopped parsley
Boiled ham	
1 skinned tomato	Salt and paprika to taste
1 bell pepper	Boiled or mayonnaise dressing
10 stuffed olives	

Put some boiled ham through a food-chopper; measure two cupfuls, and add the tomato, pepper, olives chopped fine, parsley, seasonings, and enough boiled or mayonnaise dressing to make a paste. Cut some rusks in halves and spread with the filling.

Rolled Sandwiches

1 long loaf bread	½ pint (1 cup) chopped stuffed olives
Softened butter	
1 pint (2 cups) cooked chopped ham	¼ lb. (1 cup) chopped English walnut meats

Mix the ham, olives, and nuts with enough boiled dressing to moisten them. Use a loaf that is square at the ends and one day old. Remove the crusts from the loaf and with a very sharp knife cut it into even slices, one-eighth of an inch thick. Place these slices together in the original form, wrap them in a damp cloth, and let them stand for two hours. By that time they will be soft enough to roll without breaking. Spread each slice with the softened butter and the mixture, roll it, and then wrap it in a piece of waxed paper that is wide enough to go nearly twice around it and long enough to extend beyond the roll in a twist at each end. Keep on ice until wanted.

Chicken and Cranberry Sandwiches

Buttered white bread
½ pint (1 cup) chopped
   cooked chicken
1 tablespoonful chopped
   celery
½ tablespoonful chopped
   gherkins
1 glass cranberry jelly
2 tablespoonfuls orange-
   juice

Whip up the jelly with a silver fork, add the celery, gherkins, chicken, and the orange-juice. Mix and spread on slices of buttered bread and cut into shapes. Serve in a sandwich paper holder decorated with chopped pickles.

Chicken and Ham Sandwiches

Puff pastry
½ pint (1 cup) diced
   cooked chicken
¼ pint (½ cup) diced
   cooked ham
1 hard-cooked egg,
   chopped
3 tablespoonfuls thick
   cream
2 raw egg-yolks

Mix the chicken, ham, egg, cream, raw yolks, and seasonings together, and beat them with a wooden spoon.

Roll out the pastry rather thin, and spread thickly with the mixture; cover over with pastry, brush over with a little beaten egg, mark out with a knife in any shape, and bake for fifteen minutes in a hot oven. Cut in shapes, and serve either hot or cold.

Pork and Olive Sandwiches

2 boiled pork tenderloins
¾ pint (1½ cups) stoned
  olives
1½ gills (¾ cup) milk
3 tablespoonfuls olive oil
⅓ cupful vinegar
1 teaspoonful mustard
2 eggs
Salt and pepper
Lettuce leaves

Put the well-cooked tenderloins and the olives through a food-chopper. Break the eggs into a small saucepan, stir in the mustard, add salt and pepper to taste, milk, oil, and vinegar, and stir and cook over a slow fire until the mixture comes to boiling-point. Boil for two minutes and cool. Then add the pork and olives.

Butter slices of bread, then spread the mixture on thick, and put a crisp lettuce leaf between the slices.

Pineapple Sandwiches

1 pineapple
Sugar
2 ozs. (½ cup) chopped
  preserved ginger
2 ozs. (½ cup) chopped
  maraschino cherries
White mayonnaise
Bread

Peel and slice the pineapple, add sugar to taste, and allow to stand in a cool place for three hours. Then chop fine, add ginger, cherries, and mayonnaise to moisten, and spread between thin squares of bread.

Chocolate Sandwiches

1 lb. (2 cups) sugar	2 tablespoonfuls grated chocolate
½ pint (1 cup) milk	
½ oz. (2 tablespoonfuls) flour	½ oz. (1 tablespoonful) butter
2 tablespoonfuls corn syrup	Pinch cream of tartar
Bread or cake	1 teaspoonful vanilla extract

Put into a saucepan the sugar, flour, milk, syrup and cream of tartar, stir constantly, and when it boils, add the chocolate and butter. Boil until a soft ball is formed when dropped into cold water, or until it registers 240° F., by candy thermometer. Remove from the fire, add the extract, and beat until creamy. Spread between thin rounds of cake or bread.

Another Method.—Melt two squares of chocolate over boiling water, add two tablespoonfuls of butter, one cupful of powdered sugar and three cupfuls of cream, and cook for five minutes. Add two-thirds cupful of blanched and chopped nut meats and one teaspoonful of vanilla extract. Cool before spreading between thin slices of buttered bread or cake.

Potted Beef Sandwiches

1½ lbs. lean beef	Salt and red pepper
½ lb. (1 cup) butter	4 boned anchovies
Powdered cloves and mace	Few drops red color
Powdered allspice and nutmeg	Bread

Cut the beef into tiny pieces, put it into an earthenware jar with one-half of the butter. Cover the jar, set it in a pan of boiling water, and cook. When nearly ready, add cloves, mace, allspice, nutmeg, salt, and red pepper to taste; then continue to boil it until tender and let it get cold.

Wash and bone the anchovies and pound them with the meat, the remainder of the butter, and a few drops of red color. Press into small pats and cover with melted butter or suet.

This mixture may be warmed and served with rolls or bread as a main dish.

Lady-finger Sandwiches

Stoned and chopped dates   Lemon-juice
Chopped pecan nut meats   Lady-fingers
Honey

Mix equal quantities of dates and pecan nut meats, and moisten with honey and lemon-juice to taste. Spread between lady-fingers and serve tied in small bundles. These sandwiches are appropriate with hot chocolate.

Another Method.—Spread apricot or strawberry jam between the lady-fingers. Decorate the tops with whipped and sweetened cream and candied rose leaves.

Oyster Canapés

Oysters   Lemon-juice to taste
Caviar   Buttered brown bread
Sliced cucumbers   Parsley
Salt and pepper to taste

Cut some rounds of buttered brown bread, and lay a thin slice of crisp cucumber on the top of each. Season some oysters with salt, pepper, and lemon-juice and place them on the top of the cucumber. Surround the oysters with caviar, garnish with sprigs of parsley, and serve.

Oyster Sandwiches

1 pint (2 cups) oysters   2 ozs. (4 tablespoonfuls)
1 gill (½ cup) cream   butter
2 egg-yolks   ½ teaspoonful salt
2 tablespoonfuls cracker   ¼ teaspoonful pepper
  crumbs   Buttered bread

Drain the oysters and chop them, put them into a saucepan,

cover, and let steam for five minutes; then add butter, seasonings, beaten yolks of eggs, cracker-crumbs, and cream. Cook for two minutes, set aside to cool slightly, then spread between slices of white buttered bread, and serve at once.

Onion Sandwiches

Thinly sliced onions	1 tablespoonful mustard
2 beaten eggs	1 tablespoonful sugar
1 gill (½ cup) milk	1 tablespoonful butter
1 tablespoonful salt	1 gill (½ cup) vinegar

Put the eggs in the upper pan of a double boiler, add the milk, salt, mustard, sugar, butter, and vinegar, and cook until as thick as boiled custard. Cool and spread on thin slices of bread. Put together with a layer of onions between.

Some of the large white onions of the yellow variety are not suitable for making sandwiches.

Here's a Blondie tip: Have a knife with a special colored handle for cutting onions. This makes it easily recognizable and warns against its use on other foods.

Lenten Sandwiches

1 chopped pickled beet	Mayonnaise dressing
3 small chopped pickles	Lettuce leaves
1 tablespoonful chopped capers	2 chopped hard-cooked eggs
Chopped parsley	12 thin slices bread

Put one cupful of mayonnaise dressing into a basin, add the eggs, parsley, capers, pickles, and beet. Spread a thin layer of this mixture over each slice of bread; dip some tender lettuce leaves into mayonnaise, lay them over six slices of the bread, and cover them with the other six. Trim the sandwiches all round, then cut into triangles and serve.

Lemon-butter Sandwiches

White cake   1 oz. (2 tablespoonfuls)
4 lemons   butter
1 lb. (2 cups) sugar   3 eggs

Put the grated rind of one of the lemons, with the strained juice of the four lemons, sugar, and butter into a saucepan and stir and cook for five minutes. Take from the fire and add the eggs well beaten. Return to the fire and cook for three minutes longer, stirring all the time. Be careful the mixture does not burn. Cool and spread between dainty pieces of white cake.

Or spread slices of bread with the mixture, cover, cut into fingers or any other shape preferred, and arrange daintily on a silver plate with an ornamental paper.

Cheese and Onion Sandwiches

Buttered bread   ¾ teaspoonful sugar
1½ ozs. (3 tablespoon-   1 chopped medium-sized
  fuls) butter   onion
2 tablespoonfuls French   1 teaspoonful chopped
  mustard   capers
1 tablespoonful grated   6 chopped sweet pickles
  cheese   12 chopped stuffed olives

Cream the butter, add the mustard, cheese, sugar, onion, capers, pickles, and olives. Spread between very thin slices of buttered bread and cut in squares.

Lettuce Sandwiches

Lettuce leaves   Salt, pepper, and paprika
3 onions   to taste
3 tomatoes   Vinegar
3 hard-cooked eggs   Buttered brown bread

Rub the tomatoes through a sieve. Chop the onions very fine. Mash the eggs, and add enough vinegar to make a smooth paste; then mix with the tomato and onion, and season all with salt, pepper, and paprika. Cut slices of brown bread and butter them. Lay a crisp lettuce leaf on each buttered piece; spread the above mixture over them equally, and cover with another piece of buttered brown bread. Serve on a plate covered with lettuce leaves.

Liederkranz Cheese Sandwiches

1 Liederkranz cheese	Small buttered muffins
12 stoned, chopped olives	Green onion tops

With a sharp knife cut in halves the required number of small thin muffins; butter each half, and spread over a thin layer of Liederkranz cheese. Sprinkle over with the olives and onion tops.

Liver and Chestnut Sandwiches

½ lb. (2 cups) boiled liver	1 pint (2 cups) shelled chestnuts
½ oz. (1 tablespoonful) butter	1 gill (½ cup) stock
	Buttered bread

Boil the chestnuts until soft, then blanch them and mash to a fine paste. Add the livers, chopped fine, the butter, seasonings, and stock. Heat and mix thoroughly, then set away to cool. Spread between thin slices of buttered bread. Cut into neat squares and serve.

Salmon Sandwiches

1 can salmon	⅛ teaspoonful paprika
1 oz. (2 tablespoonfuls) butter	1 gill (½ cup) vinegar
½ oz. (2 tablespoonfuls) flour	½ pint (1 cup) milk or cream
2 teaspoonfuls sugar	2 egg-yolks
1 teaspoonful salt	Buttered bread
1 teaspoonful mustard	½ tablespoonful lemon-juice

Sprinkle the lemon-juice over the salmon. Melt the butter in a saucepan, stir in the flour, add the seasonings, milk or cream, and when smooth add the vinegar. Stir until thick and pour on the beaten yolks of eggs; return to the fire and cook for a few minutes. Do not curdle the eggs, add the salmon, and cool.

Spread between slices of buttered bread and cut into square pieces.

One-half cupful of chopped peanuts may be added to the salmon mixture if liked.

Sardine Canapés

8 sardines	2 teaspoonfuls chopped
2 tablespoonfuls lemon-juice	parsley
	2 ozs. (4 tablespoonfuls)
½ teaspoonful Worcester-shire sauce	butter
	2 hard-cooked eggs
⅛ teaspoonful paprika	Capers or watercress

Toast lightly oval-shaped slices of bread. Skin and bone the sardines, rub them to a paste, add the seasonings and the butter creamed. Spread this mixture on the canapés, garnish with a border of the egg-whites, finely chopped, and on the top scatter the yolks of eggs rubbed through a ricer, and a few capers or sprigs of watercress.

Sardine and Anchovy Sandwiches

12 sardines	1 teaspoonful chopped
6 anchovies	parsley
4 ozs. (½ cup) butter	Salt and paprika to taste

Remove the skin and bones from the anchovies and sardines and pound them; add the butter, parsley, salt, and paprika, and mix well together; cut some thin white bread and butter it; spread freely with the sardine mixture, cover with a slice of buttered bread, trim off the crusts, and cut into fingers. Decorate with sprigs of parsley and serve on a sandwich tray.

A pleasing sandwich filling can be made by mashing twelve boned sardines with a cream cheese and a little of their own oil. Season with red pepper and finely chopped parsley.

Anchovies may be substituted for the sardines, and paprika and mint used for seasonings.

Marmalade and Nut Sandwiches

24 blanched and chopped almonds

24 blanched and chopped English walnut meats

1 pint (2 cups) orange or grapefruit marmalade

White or graham bread buttered

Mix the nuts with the marmalade and spread on thin slices of buttered white or graham bread.

Almond Sandwiches

Buttered white or brown bread

Almond paste

Glacé fruits

Red currant jelly

Parsley (or watercress) sprigs

1 egg-white

Butter some thin slices of white or brown bread. Beat up the white of egg and with it thin some almond paste. Spread between the slices of bread. Decorate the top with the red currant jelly, putting it through a small bag and tube, small pieces of glacé fruits, and leaves of parsley. Cut into finger-shaped pieces.

Lobster Sandwiches

Slices bread	Chopped parsley
Sweet butter	Capers
Salt and paprika	Liquid aspic jelly
Hard-cooked egg-yolk	Lettuce or watercress
Pounded cooked lobster	leaves

Spread some thinly cut slices of bread with sweet butter, sprinkle this with a little salt and paprika, and on this sprinkle some hard-cooked yolk of egg which has been rubbed through a wire sieve.

Have some more buttered bread spread with the lobster, and sprinkled with chopped parsley and capers. Close the slices together, the last mentioned on the top, then cut out with a round cutter about two inches in diameter. Brush over the top side of the rounds with a little liquid aspic jelly and sprinkle with chopped parsley.

Place the lettuce or watercress in the center of a dish, and arrange the sandwiches round the salad. Potted lobster may be used.

Another Method.—Remove meat from a boiled lobster and slice into small pieces. Cut bread thin, remove crusts, and butter. Mix the lobster with mayonnaise dressing and spread thinly between two slices of bread. Cut into oblong pieces.

Sunday Night Canapés

1 finnan haddie	Grated Parmesan cheese
2 tablespoonfuls cream	Brown breadcrumbs
1 oz. (2 tablespoonfuls)	Fried croûtons
sweet butter	1 teaspoonful lemon-juice

Soak the haddie in milk and water for thirty minutes, then cook it, drain, and rub through a sieve. Melt the butter in a saucepan, add seasonings, cream, and sieved haddie. When hot, pile on fried croûtons, sprinkle with cheese mixed with a few breadcrumbs, return to the oven for a minute, and serve very hot.

Maple Sandwiches

½ pint (1 cup) maple syrup

1 gill (½ cup) stoned chopped dates

1 gill (½ cup) blanched, chopped almonds

1 gill (½ cup) diced pine-apple

1 tablespoonful crushed maple sugar

Buttered bread

Put the maple syrup into a saucepan, add the dates, almonds and pineapple and cook gently for eight minutes. Take from the fire and add the maple sugar.

Cut the bread in long, thin slices, and remove the crusts. Spread with the mixture, and roll up, wrapping each in waxed paper. Let stand for a few hours, when the paper can be removed and they will keep the shape desired.

Another Method.—Mix one cupful of grated maple sugar with one cupful of blanched and chopped almonds and mix to a paste with whipped cream; spread on buttered white or Graham bread and cut into shapes. Decorate with chopped almonds, and serve around a mound of molded cream-cheese balls flecked with paprika.

Mint Sandwiches

8 large sprigs mint

½ pint (1 cup) boiling water

1 pint (2 cups) whipped cream

4 tablespoonfuls cold water

1 oz. (3 tablespoonfuls) powdered gelatine

Bread

Chop the mint, put it into a saucepan with the boiling water, and simmer for thirty minutes. Soak the gelatine in the cold water and add to mint, and after this dissolves, strain. When nearly cold, add the whipped cream and mix well. When cold, spread on bread.

Another Method.—To four tablespoonfuls of finely chopped mint add four tablespoonfuls of chopped parsley, four teaspoonfuls of chopped chives, paprika to taste, and enough mayonnaise dressing to mix. Spread upon thin slices of fine-grained white bread.

Tango Sandwiches

Thin dry toast
Anchovy purée
Chopped parsley or
  chopped pistachio nuts
4 hard-cooked egg-yolks
2 ozs. (4 tablespoonfuls)
  sweet butter

2 boned anchovies
1 tablespoonful potted
  fish
1 tablespoonful thick
  white sauce
Salt and paprika to taste
Few drops red color

Pound the yolks of eggs with the butter, anchovies, and potted fish. Add the sauce, red color, and salt and paprika, and rub through a wire sieve. Have some very thin dry toast made, and, while hot, spread it with some of the above mixture. Lay two pieces of toast together to make a sandwich, cut them into neat squares or oblong shapes, spread the top sides lightly with anchovy purée, and on this put a good sprinkling of chopped parsley or pistachio nuts. These are excellent for afternoon tea.

To make the anchovy purée: Take eight large anchovies that have been boned and well washed in cold water; add to them two hard-cooked yolks of eggs, four tablespoonfuls of sweet butter, paprika to taste, and a few drops of red color, and pound all together; rub through a wire sieve and use.

Mushroom and Lobster Sandwiches

1 can or (1 cup) cooked
  lobster meat
½ pint (1 cup) mush-
  rooms
1 oz. (2 tablespoonfuls)
  butter

Stock
Salt and pepper to taste
Tomato ketchup to taste
Lemon-juice to taste
White bread
1 small onion

Wash and dry the mushrooms and cut them into small pieces. Melt the butter in a saucepan, add the onion chopped and the mushrooms, cover with stock, and cook slowly until tender. Drain the mushrooms, add the lobster meat to them, and pound until smooth; add seasonings and enough of the liquor to moisten. Spread on thin buttered slices of white bread.

Marshmallow Sandwiches

Marshmallows   Buttered bread

Cut some marshmallows in halves and place them between small narrow fingers of buttered bread; then toast in a very hot oven, first on one side and then on the other.

Halibut Sandwiches

1 pint (2 cups) cold cooked halibut
2 hard-cooked eggs
2 tablespoonfuls chopped capers

1 tablespoonful lemon-juice
Mayonnaise dressing
Radishes
Lightly buttered bread

Shred the fish and chop the hard-cooked eggs. Mix these with the capers, add the lemon-juice, and moisten with mayonnaise dressing. Spread on slices of lightly buttered bread, cover with other slices, and cut into fancy shapes. Serve with the radishes.

Pattern Sandwich

1 cream cheese
2½ tablespoonfuls peanut butter

1 chopped pimiento
Salt and paprika to taste
White and graham bread

Mash the cheese and mix it with the peanut butter, pimiento, salt, and paprika to taste.

Cut three slices each of white and graham bread, one-half inch thick. Spread a slice of the white bread with mixture and place a slice of graham bread upon it. Spread this with mixture and place on it a slice of white bread. Repeat this process, beginning with the slice of graham bread. Put both piles in a cold place under a light weight for one hour. Remove the weight, and cut each pile in three and one-half inch slices. Spread two of them with the prepared mixture, and put together in such a way that a white block is alternately with a graham one, making a checker appearance. Wrap in **damp** cheesecloth and again place under a light weight in a cool place. Remove the weight at serving time and cut in dice.

Tongue Canapés

Cooked tongue	Paprika
Buttered brown bread	Grated horseradish
1 peeled and sliced tomato	Tarragon vinegar
Whipped cream	

Cut some rounds of buttered brown bread. Place a thin slice of tomato on each canapé, and cover with a thin round of tongue. Whip up some cream, seasoning to taste with the vinegar and horseradish, and pile a little of this on each round of tongue. Sprinkle with paprika and serve on a lace-edged paper.

Pâté de Foie Gras Sandwiches

Pâté de foie gras (1 jar or tin)	Oil
	Vinegar
Brown or white bread	Salt and pepper to taste
Butter	Parsley
Cucumbers	

Cut some thin slices of buttered bread and stamp out rounds from them the size of the rounds of cucumber. Peel and slice the cucumbers and let them lie for a short time in a dressing made of salt, vinegar, oil, and pepper, then drain.

Spread one-half of the slices with pâté de foie gras, lay on a slice of cucumber, place the other slice of bread on the top, and arrange in a ring in a dish, the sandwiches overlapping each other. Garnish with parsley.

Or spread pâté de foie gras on lightly buttered bread, cover with a layer of chopped watercress mixed with French dressing, place slices of bread on the top, and cut into finger-shaped pieces, and pile log-cabin fashion in a sandwich basket.

Pâté de foie gras mixed with truffles is delicious and delicate.

Nasturtium Sandwiches

Nasturtium flowers   Buttered bread, brown or
Salt and pepper to taste   white

Chop some nasturtium flowers, season with salt and a little pepper, spread on a slice of bread and butter very thinly cut, cover, and cut into any desired shape, and decorate the sandwiches with a few nasturtium blooms. Or flavor some butter with nasturtium leaves and blossoms, and with it spread a thin slice of moist bread. Press fresh nasturtium leaves and blossoms upon the butter, and place one piece of bread upon the other. These sandwiches may be modified by combining thin slices of cucumber with the blossoms. The leaves also make a capital addition to ordinary chopped or sliced meat or egg sandwiches, and may be recommended to those in search of something new for afternoon teas or picnics.

Nut and Honey Sandwiches

1 gill (½ cup) honey   ½ lb. (1 cup) butter
3 ozs. (¾ cup) chopped   Biscuits or crackers
   black walnut meats

Melt the butter, stir in the honey and the walnuts. Chill and spread between crackers or biscuits. To make honey sandwiches for afternoon tea cut thin slices of brown or entire wheat bread and spread quite thick with honey. Sprinkle with chopped preserved cherries or chopped preserved ginger, and press the slices together. Cut into fancy shapes and serve.

Nut Canapés

¼ lb. (1 cup) chopped   6 chopped sweet pickles
   nut meats   Bread
Mayonnaise dressing   Pimientoes

Mix the nut meats and the pickles with enough mayonnaise dressing to spread. Fry circles of bread in hot fat and spread with the nut mixture. Garnish with stars of pimientoes.

Olive Sandwiches

6 hard-cooked eggs
½ pint (1 cup) stuffed
  olives
Buttered bread

½ pint (1 cup) English
  walnut meats
Mayonnaise or boiled
  dressing

Chop the eggs, nuts, and olives separately, then mix them together and moisten with the dressing. Spread between thin slices of buttered bread and cut into fancy shapes.

New England Sandwiches

Graham and white bread
½ pint (1 cup) chopped
  nut meats
2 lemons
½ pound stoned dates

½ lb. seeded raisins
¾ lb. of figs
12 marshmallows
1 oz. (2 tablespoonfuls)
  sugar
1 beaten egg white

Put the figs, dates, and raisins through a food-chopper, add the strained juice of the lemon, the sugar, nut meats, the marshmallows melted, and white of egg. Mix and spread on rounds of graham and white bread.

Sardine and Tomato Sandwiches

1 can sardines
2 ozs. (4 tablespoonfuls)
  butter
Salt

Red pepper
Buttered bread
Skinned tomatoes
Lemon-juice

Skin and bone the sardines and pound them with the butter, seasoning to taste with salt and red pepper. Spread this mixture on thin rounds of buttered bread; cut the tomatoes the same size as rounds of bread, and place a slice between two pieces, first squeezing a little lemon-juice over them. Press the rounds firmly together.

Another Method.—Skin and bone one can of sardines. Beat up one egg, add one-fourth cupful of milk and one-fourth teaspoonful of salt. Dip twelve slices of French bread in the egg mixture, and fry quickly in plenty of smoking hot fat. Place a sardine between each two slices of the fried bread, garnish with a slice of hard-cooked egg and a sprig of parsley. Serve at once.

Savory Cream Sandwiches

1 gill (½ cup) whipped cream	Unbuttered bread
	Salt and pepper to taste
2 teaspoonfuls anchovy extract or shrimp paste	Beaten egg-white or liquid aspic jelly
1 teaspoonful finely chopped parsley	Paprika

Mix the cream with the anchovy extract, parsley, salt and pepper to taste. Spread on slices of unbuttered bread and cut into squares or triangles; brush the edges with beaten white of egg or liquid aspic jelly, and dust these with chopped parsley and paprika.

Shad Roe Sandwich

4 ozs. (½ cup) butter	3 drops tabasco sauce
3 hard-cooked egg-yolks	3 chopped olives
1 cooked shad roe	Salt and paprika to taste

Pound the roe and rub it through a sieve with the hard-cooked yolks of eggs. Cream the butter, add all the other ingredients, then spread between slices of bread. Cut into shapes and dish up neatly on a sandwich tray.

Cooked cod's roe may be used in place of the shad roe.

Another Method.—Crush a pair of cooked shad roes with a silver fork and moisten with mayonnaise dressing flavored with tarragon vinegar. Spread one slice of white bread lightly with mayonnaise dressing and cover with chopped watercress; spread the second slice with butter, and then with the shad-roe mixture, and press lightly together.

Sausage Sandwiches

Smoked pork sausage	Sliced gherkins
White or brown bread	Butter or
French mustard	margarine

Cut very thinly the required number of slices of smoked ham sausage. Butter some thinly cut slices of brown or white bread, spread over each a little mustard, and then add a layer of thinly sliced gherkins. Lay the slices of sausage between each two slices of buttered bread, and trim and cut into the desired shapes.

SOUPS

"I THOUGHT Blondie might like a little chicken broth, Dagwood; I hear she has a cold," said Mrs. Finney at the door, handing over a covered cook-pot. "We all have colds," he told her, and thanked her for her neighborliness.

Dagwood carried the large vessel upstairs to Blondie.

"Look, Dear, look at the lovely chicken broth Mrs. Finney sent over."

Alexander, running up the stairs, interrupted with a shout, "Daddy, quick, your water's boiling all over the stove!"

"I'll be right back, Dear," called Dagwood as he hastened to the kitchen. "And I'll bring you a dish and spoon."

"Did Mrs. Finney send enough soup for us too?" queried Alexander as Dagwood finished his work at the stove.

"Plenty," answered Dagwood.

On his return to Blondie's room, Dagwood carried another large cooking vessel. "Here, Dear, I made you a nice hot mustard footbath to take away your chill," he said.

"How nice," replied Blondie, "will you hand me my robe out of the closet please? "I'll have the footbath first. You can take the broth down and eat some."

It was a short time later that Alexander and Dagwood seated themselves at the kitchen table prepared for a feast on Mrs. Finney's soup.

After the first spoonful, Alexander turned to his father with an expression of horror. "This soup is terrible, I can't eat it," he exclaimed.

Dagwood tasted it too, and in a few seconds he was back upstairs carrying the cookpot.

"Oh, Dagwood, this hot foot bath is simply wonderful," said Blondie as Dagwood entered the room.

"It should be!" replied Dagwood, "It's Mrs. Finney's chicken broth. I took the wrong cookpot downstairs."

You won't make a mistake with soups in this book. When the directions are followed with the loving care that soup deserves, its aroma is mouth-watering and unmistakable. There's no appetizer for any meal as good as a cup of soup. And a big pot of soup can be the main dish for any luncheon or dinner.

Foundation Soup Stock

2½ to 3 lbs. shin or shank of beef with meat and marrow bone	3 sprigs parsley
	½ cup diced celery and leaves
3 quarts water	10 peppercorns
1 onion, sliced	1 tablespoon salt

Wipe meat and bone with dampened cloth, and cut meat in cubes. Put one-half meat cubes into soup kettle, cover with cold water and heat slowly to the simmering point, just below boiling. Scrape the marrow from the bone, putting it into a large frying pan and melt over low heat. Add remaining half of meat cubes and brown on all sides, then put with bone into soup kettle. Cover and simmer for 5 hours. At the end of that time, add vegetables and seasonings, cover kettle and cook two hours longer. During this cooking time, if more water is needed, add boiling water so as not to stop the cooking. If soup is to be served immediately, skim off the top, and serve with meat and vegetables, with hot toast or crackers. If it is not to be used until next day, omit vegetables and last 2 hours of cooking, chill thoroughly, skim off fat, add vegetables and cook the last two hours next day. Be sure it is seasoned to taste, and serve piping hot. Add as many vegetables as you like —potatoes, diced celery, tomatoes, carrots, turnips and onions.

Beef and Vegetable Chowder

½ cup sliced onion
½ cup chopped green
  pepper
¼ cup butter or marga-
  rine
1 pound ground beef
3 cups sliced potatoes
5 cups boiling water

2 cups cooked or canned
  tomatoes
3 teaspoons salt
⅛ teaspoon pepper
3½ tablespoons flour
½ teaspoon chili powder
5 tablespoons cold water

This is not Mrs. Murphy's chowder, so no overalls are necessary.

Saute the onion and green pepper in butter until the onion is lightly yellowed. Add meat and cook, stirring frequently, until the meat is lightly browned. Cook the potatoes in boiling water until tender. Add the beef mixture and tomatoes, salt and pepper and bring to a boil. Combine the flour and chili powder with the cold water and blend well. Add to the cooked mixture and simmer until slightly thickened.

Beef Shank Barley Soup

2 lbs. beef shank
2 cups water
1 teaspoon salt
⅛ teaspoon pepper
⅓ cup diced celery
⅓ cup diced or sliced
  carrots
⅓ cup chopped onions

⅛ teaspoon cayenne
2 tablespoons chopped
  parsley
1 qt. soup stock or bul-
  lion
3 tablespoons barley
½ teaspoon Worcester-
  shire sauce

Add water and seasonings to beef shank and simmer about 2 hours or until meat is tender. Pick meat from bones and return meat to stock. Add vegetables, soup stock and barley and simmer 25 to 30 minutes, add Worcestershire sauce and serve. Serves 5. Another method of making this soup is to completely cover meat with water and simmer the requisite amount of time until meat is tender. If this is done, there will be enough soup without adding stock. Different vegetables may be used such as celery, turnips, etc., as many as your ingenuity can suggest and in various combinations.

Bean Soup

Ham bones or butt	Celery stalk or leaves
1 onion	Salt
1 cup navy beans	Pepper

Wash and soak 1 cup navy beans overnight or for several hours. Put ham bones in saucepan, add onion, cut up, celery or leaves, cover well with cold water and cook 2 hours at simmering temperature. Put in strainer and press as much of the vegetables through as possible. Add beans and simmer gently until beans are very soft, season with salt and pepper and serve.

Celery Soup

1 tablespoon margarine	Liquid in which celery is
1 tablespoon flour	cooked
½ cup celery, cut in ½	1 pint milk
inch pieces	Salt and pepper

Wash and cut up celery, cook in a little boiling salted water until tender, about 10 min.; then drain but save liquid. Melt margarine, blend in flour, gradually add milk and celery water and bring to a boil, stirring constantly. When smooth and at boiling point, add celery and season. Serves 4.

Chicken Soup

1 chicken	1 sprig parsley
4 quarts water	1 teaspoon salt
1 onion	6 pepper corns
3 stalks celery	¾ cup rice

Dress and cut fowl in pieces and put into a saucepan. Add water, cover and bring to the boiling point. Reduce heat and simmer slowly three hours. Add onion, celery, parsley, salt and peppercorns. Cook one hour longer. Take out fowl, strain stock and cool. Remove fat when cold. Cut 1½ cups meat from the breast in small cubes and add to soup. Steam the rice in two cups water in a double boiler about 30 minutes. Add to soup. Add more seasoning if necessary.

Clam Chowder

50 clams	7 large potatoes
½ lb. fat salt pork	½ cup flour
1 qt. can tomatoes	1 cup cold water to dissolve flour
8 medium sized onions	Seasoning to taste

Grind or chip the pork and fry, but do not brown it; add the chopped onions, then the tomatoes and put in six quarts of water. Boil slowly for three to four hours, add the potatoes, cut into dice, and cook a half hour longer. A half hour before removing from the fire stir in the flour and water, and ten minutes before taking from the fire put in the clams and their liquor.

Cream of Asparagus Soup

1 can asparagus ends	1 teaspoon salt
2 cups milk	2 tablespoons margarine
2 tablespoons flour	Dash pepper or paprika

Do not drain asparagus. Melt margarine, add flour and mix smooth, then gradually add milk, stirring constantly until smooth and slightly thickened, add can of asparagus, season with pepper and salt, and taste to see if it is seasoned correctly.

Angelemono Soup

10 cups of chicken or lamb broth	2 lemons (juice)
4 eggs	1 cup of rice
	1 teaspoon of salt

Take lamb or chicken and boil for about two hours to make the broth. Strain broth and add cup of rice which has been washed. Let boil for about twenty minutes. While the rice is boiling whip the four eggs for about three minutes. Add the lemon juice stirring constantly and continue to stir until thoroughly mixed. Strain half the rice from the broth and stir into the egg mixture. Then slowly add the egg mixture to the broth and remains of the rice, stirring all the while. No further cooking is needed. Serve piping hot. Serves 8 persons.

Cream of Chicken and Corn Soup

2 teaspoons butter or margarine	1 can milk
2 teaspoons flour	3 tablespoons cooked corn
1 can chicken soup	3 tablespoons chopped fresh tomato

Melt butter or fat, add flour and cook over a low heat until frothy. Add milk and cook until thickened, then add soup and corn and heat, but do not boil. Add chopped tomatoes just before serving. Serves 3 or 4.

Cream of Carrot Soup

2 cups carrots, grated	2 tablespoons butter
1 small onion, grated	1 qt. foundation stock
1 tablespoon sugar	1 cup evaporated milk o:
1 teaspoon salt	1 cup bottle milk
½ cup bread crumbs	½ cup water

Combine carrot, onion, sugar, salt and water and cook for about 5 minutes or until carrots are tender. Add butter, bread crumbs and broth, and simmer for 20 minutes. Add milk and cook 5 minutes longer or until thoroughly heated. Serve at once. Serves 6. Four bouillon cubes in 1 qt. boiling water will make 1 qt. of broth, if you do not have foundation stock, which every good soup maker keeps supplied with.

Cream of Mushroom

1 lb. mushrooms	2 tablespoons flour
¼ cup melted butter	1 cup cream
1 qt. milk	Salt
2 slices onion	Pepper

Wash and skin mushrooms, chop fine and saute for about 10 minutes in 2 tablespoons butter. Heat milk in double boiler with onion. Blend remaining butter with flour, add to milk and cook until thickened. Remove onion, stir in mushrooms and cream, and season with salt and pepper. Serve hot with chopped parsley over top. Serves 6.

Cream of Spinach Soup

4 cups milk	2 tablespoons fat
2 tablespoons flour	Salt, pepper and other
2 cups spinach pulp and water	seasonings

Wash thoroughly and cook 1 lb. fresh spinach or use frozen spinach. Rub through a sieve and save the small amount of water in which it was cooked. Make a white sauce of the liquid, flour and fat; add the spinach and water, season to taste and serve.

Cream of Vegetable Soup

2 tablespoons butter	2 cups milk
1 slice onion	1½ cups pureed vegetables
1 piece celery	Salt, pepper to taste
1 tablespoon flour	

Melt butter in pan, put in onion and celery and cook over a very low heat 3 minutes, taking care that neither the butter nor vegetables brown or burn. Remove onion and celery, blend in flour; add milk gradually, stirring in carefully, to prevent lumping.

Add strained vegetables slowly, blending well. Heat together and season. Serves 4.

Other vegetables may also be used this way.

Kidney Bean and Rice Soup

1 pint kidney beans	3 sliced onions
2 quarts water	2 stalks celery
2 small carrots, finely chopped	1 cup cooked rice
Salt and pepper	2 tablespoons butter

Wash and soak beans over night; drain. Add all of the other ingredients except rice, salt, pepper and butter and cook until beans are very soft. Rub through colander, add cooked rice, and heat to boiling point. Add butter, salt and pepper to serve. Other beans or lentils may be substituted for the kidney beans. Serves 8.

Cream of Corn Soup

Leftover corn on cob	1 tablespoon flour
1 tablespoon butter	1 pt. milk
Pepper	Salt

Cut corn from cob. Melt butter in saucepan, add flour and blend, then gradually add milk, stirring until thickened; add corn. Season with a dash of pepper and ½ teaspoon salt.

Fish Chowder

2 cups flaked fresh fish	3 potatoes cubed
3 cups water	2 tablespoons flour
2 large onions, diced	1¾ cup milk or light
2 tablespoons fat	cream
2 tablespoons salt	Dash pepper or paprika

Heat water, add flaked fish and heat to boiling; drain, saving stock. Melt 1 tablespoon fat in soup pot, saute onions slowly until tender; cover. Combine fish stock and onions, add potatoes and cook 10 to 15 minutes, until potatoes are tender. In a separate pan melt the other tablespoon of fat, blend in flour, add milk. Continue cooking, stirring constantly; add mixture and reheat. Serves 6.

Jellied Chicken Broth

2 envelopes plain, un- flavored gelatin	¼ teaspoon celery salt
3 cups chicken broth	1 tablespoon lemon juice
¼ teaspoon salt	1 tablespoon onion juice

Soften gelatin in cold water and dissolve in hot broth; add salt, celery salt, lemon and onion juice. Pour into bouillon cups that have been rinsed in cold water and chill. This soup may be served hot if preferred. Serves 6.

Lentil Soup

1 cup lentils	4 cups stock
1 carrot	4 tablespoons flour
1 stock celery	4 teaspoons butter
1 onion	2 teaspoons salt

Soak lentils in water several hours, then drain and cut onion, carrot and celery fine. Place in stove 7 hours. Remove and rub through sieve. Make paste of flour, add flour, stock and seasoning. Heat and serve. To cream Lentil Soup add one quart of milk instead of stock.

Pot-Luck Soup

Tops and tough stalks of celery	1 med. size potato
1 carrot cut fine	1 cup milk
1 onion	½ tablespoon flour
1 tablespoon butter	Salt, pepper, paprika

Cut stalks of celery and leaves into pieces, add cut carrot, onion and potato, and cover with cold water. Cook gently until all are very tender, then put through wire strainer, getting as much of the vegetables through the strainer as possible. Save the water in which vegetables are cooked. Melt margarine or butter in saucepan, add flour and slowly stir in milk. When it comes to boiling point add vegetables and water in which they were cooked, season and serve hot.

Oyster Soup

1 pint oysters	1 tablespoon butter or
2 cups milk	margarine

Put milk and butter over low heat. Pick oysters over carefully for bits of shell; strain liquor and save. When milk comes to boiling point, add oysters and strained liquor and let cook for 5 minutes, or until edges of oysters curl. Season well with salt and pepper, and serve piping hot. Serves 2 or 3.

Philadelphia Pepper Pot

1 beef bone or veal knuckle	¼ red pepper
	¼ lb. tripe
¼ cup onion	2 potatoes
1 bay leaf	Salt, pepper
1 stalk celery	Cayenne pepper

Cover large, uncooked bone with water and simmer slowly for 3 or 4 hours, then cool. Skim off fat and strain stock. If necessary add water to make about 6 cups stock. Add onion, bay leaf, celery, red pepper and tripe, all chopped, simmer slowly 1 hour. Season with pepper, salt and dash of cayenne. Serves 6.

Minestrone

1 cup dried beans	⅛ lb. lean salt pork
1 quart water	1 white turnip, cut fine
1 large onion, sliced thin	1 summer squash, peeled
2 tablespoons bacon fat	and diced
3 large tomatoes	⅛ teaspoon thyme
3 carrots	1 laurel leaf
½ small head cabbage	Salt and pepper
shredded	2 cups hot water

Soak beans over night, cook in the quart of water until tender. Brown onion in bacon fat; add salt pork cut in tiny squares, combine with rest of the ingredients; add to beans and cook one hour, adding water if necessary. Serve with breadsticks and grated cheese. Serves 8.

Mock Turtle Soup

1 calf's liver and heart	Salt, pepper, ground cloves
1 knuckle veal	4 yolks, hardboiled eggs
1 chopped onion	Slice of lemon

To calf's liver and heart, add knuckle of veal, cover with water and place on stove for five hours. Strain off, chop meat fine, add cloves to taste, thickening if necessary with a little browned flour, cooking a few minutes in liquor. Have yolks of four hard-boiled eggs cut up for tureen, also slices of lemon. Leave in stove five hours.

Mulligatawny

1½ lbs. lean mutton	1 dessertspoonful curry
2 ozs. (4 tablespoonfuls)	powder
butter or drippings	1 teaspoonful curry paste
3 pints (6 cups) cold	1½ ozs. (6 tablespoonfuls)
water or stock	flour
2 onions	½ pint (1 cup) hot milk
1 sour apple	1 tablespoonful chutney
4 tablespoonfuls chopped	1 bunch herbs
ham	Salt and pepper to taste
½ small carrot	1 lemon
½ small turnip	Boiled rice

Wipe the meat and cut it in small pieces. Melt the butter or drippings in a saucepan, add to it the apple and vegetables cut in small pieces, and cook for five minutes over the fire. Add the curry powder, curry paste, chutney and flour, and mix well; then add the water or stock, meat, herbs, salt and pepper. Stir over the fire for five minutes and then simmer for two hours, skimming when necessary. When ready, strain through a fine sieve into a basin. Lift out the best pieces of the meat for serving in the soup and rub as much as possible of the remainder through the sieve.

Rinse out the saucepan and return the soup to it with the meat. Season carefully, add one tablespoonful of lemon juice and the hot milk just before serving. Serve the soup with plain boiled rice. If liked a lemon cut in quarters may also be handed.

The addition of a little cream is a great improvement to this soup.

Okra Soup

24 small okra, sliced	1 minced onion
1 quart stock	1 pint strained tomatoes

Into one quart of stock that has been freed from grease, stir one minced onion and the cleaned okra, cut into thin slices. Stew until okra is tender, add one pint of strained tomatoes and season to taste.

Mushroom Broth

2 envelopes plain, un-flavored gelatin	½ a thinly sliced onion
½ cup cold water	½ stalk chopped celery
4 cups soup stock	½ teaspoon salt
¾ cup mushrooms broken into pieces	⅛ teaspoon pepper
	1 clove

Soften gelatin in cold water. Mix soup stock, mushrooms and seasoning in saucepan and boil slowly 10 minutes. Dissolve gelatin in hot stock, strain and chill. Serve cold with lemon slices or quarters. Chicken stock, beef stock, canned soup or bouillon cubes may be used in this recipe. Serves 6.

Onion Soup

2 cups finely chopped onions	1½ qts. hot meat broth
	Salt and pepper
2 tablespoons fat	3 tablespoons flour

Cook finely chopped onions in fat until lightly browned; sprinkle with flour and stir. Add hot meat broth made by cooking a soup bone in water, and stir until smooth. Season with salt and pepper and simmer until onions are tender and flavor well blended. Serve in bowls with a slice of toast in each. A little dry grated cheese on top of the toast is nice.

Potato Soup

3 small potatoes	½ teaspoon salt
1 pint milk	Dash of pepper
1 teaspoon chopped onion	Pinch cayenne
Stalk of celery	½ tablespoon flour
½ teaspoon celery salt	1 tablespoon butter

Boil potatoes in a little water until soft, drain and mash, saving the liquid. Cook onion and celery in the milk, add to mashed potatoes, rub through strainer. Boil again, thicken with flour and butter mixed together and added, stirring constantly, season. Boil 5 minutes, and serve. More milk may be added if this is too thick.

Potato Chowder

2 slices salt pork	4 cups scalded milk
1 sliced onion	Salt and pepper
2 cups diced potatoes	3 tablespoons butter
1 cup corn	6 soda crackers

Cut pork in small pieces and fry until crisp. Remove bits of pork. Add onion and cook slowly for five minutes. Do not brown. Parboil potatoes for five minutes in water to cover. Add potatoes to fat with two cups of water in which they were cooked. Cook until potatoes are tender, then add corn and milk. Season with salt, pepper and butter. Pour over crackers in soup plates and sprinkle with bits of salt pork. Serves 6.

Potato and Onion Soup

6 small white onions	2½ cups potatoes
1 cup celery	1½ tablespoons flour
5 tablespoons butter	Salt, pepper, cayenne,
1 quart milk	minced parsley

Cut the onions and celery in thin slices and saute in 3 tablespoons butter, stirring constantly until clear and yellow. Add the milk and cook altogether in the top of a double boiler for three quarters of an hour. Cut the potatoes in small dice and cook them until softened in boiling salted water—about 10 minutes. Blend 2 tablespoons butter with the flour over the flame, add the milk, vegetables and the potatoes. Cook together until all is soft and thick, season well and serve with minced parsley on top. Yield: 4 to 6 portions.

Onion Soup with Cheese

3 oz. grated cheese	1 quart boiling water
4 small onions	1 teaspoon salt
3 tablespoons shortening	⅛ teaspoon pepper
1 tablespoon flour	10 rounds toasted bread

Slice onions thinly and brown in shortening; add flour and cook 2 minutes. Add boiling water and seasoning, and boil 10 minutes. Cut bread in ⅓ inch slices, shape into rounds with a biscuit cutter. Place rounds of bread in hot soup tureen or individual soup plates and pour boiling mixture over them. Toasted rye bread may be used. Sprinkle 1 ounce grated Italian cheese over top. Remaining cheese should be served in a separate dish to be added to soup as desired. Serves 6.

Quick Turnip Soup

1 quart milk	2 tablespoons melted
1 onion, cut in half	butter
1 tablespoon flour	2 cups grated, raw turnip
1 teaspoon salt	Chopped parsley

Heat milk in double boiler with onion; add flour and fat, which have been well blended, then the turnip and salt. Cook until turnip is tender, or for about 10 minutes, and remove onion. Sprinkle chopped parsley over soup just before serving. Serves 6.

Split Pea Soup

1 ham bone	½ onion
1 lb. split peas	Salt
2 carrots	Pepper

Cover cooked ham bone with water; simmer slowly 2 hours, remove bone and add any meat clinging to bone to soup stock. Add peas; scrub carrots and dice. Chop onion, and add carrot and onion to stock. Cover and simmer slowly 1 hour, then add salt and pepper to taste. Serves 6.

Tomato Consomme

1 quart can tomatoes	½ slice onion
1 cup water	2 cloves
2 stalks celery	3 or 4 peppercorns
1 small carrot	Small blade mace
2 tablespoons chopped green pepper	½ teaspoon salt
	⅛ teaspoon pepper

Combine ingredients in a saucepan, heat to simmering point and simmer 15 minutes. Strain, season to taste and serve piping hot.

Tomato Soup

2 envelopes plain, un-flavored gelatin	2 whole cloves
½ cup cold water	2 tablespoons chopped onion
2½ cups meat stock	2 tablespoons chopped parsley
1 cup tomatoes	

Soften gelatin in cold water; mix stock, tomatoes, onion, parsley, salt and cloves, and simmer until onion is tender. Add gelatin to hot soup and stir thoroughly. Strain. Heat to boiling and serve hot, or pour into bouillon cups and chill thoroughly. Serves 6.

Potato and Corn Chowder

3 tablespoons chopped bacon	2 tablespoons flour
4 tablespoons chopped onion	1½ teaspoons salt
2 cups diced raw potatoes	¼ teaspoons pepper
2 cups water	4 cups milk
3 tablespoons butter	2 cups grated carrot
	2 cups canned corn
	½ teaspoon paprika

Brown bacon and onion in frying pan. Add potato and water and cook until potatoes are tender (about 20 minutes). Melt butter in saucepan over low heat, add flour and seasoning, mixing well. Add milk and cook until slightly thickened. Add corn, carrot and potato mixture. Heat and serve. 4 to 6 portions.

Tomato Bisque Soup

4 cups milk	2 cups, raw or canned tomatoes
¾ cup stale bread crumbs	⅓ teaspoon soda
½ onion stick with 6 cloves	½ teaspoon salt
Sprig parsley	⅛ teaspoon pepper
Bit of bay leaf	⅓ cup butter or margarine
2 teaspoons sugar	

Scald milk with bread crumbs, onion, parsley and bay leaf. Remove seasonings and rub through a seive. Cook tomatoes with sugar 15 minutes, add soda and rub through seive. Reheat bread and milk to boiling point, add tomatoes, and pour at once into tureen over butter, salt and pepper. Serve with croutons or crackers. Serves 6.

Watercress and Cheese Soup

2 tablespoons butter	3 cups milk
2 tablespoons flour	4 oz. processed cheese cut in small pieces
¼ teaspoon salt	1 cup chopped watercress
Pepper	

Melt butter in top of double boiler; stir in flour and salt.

Place over boiling water; add milk gradually. Cook slowly, stirring constantly, until thickened. Add cheese and continue cooking until cheese has melted. Stir in watercress and cook 5 minutes. Serves 4.

Vegetable Thrift Soup

Bones and leftover meat	Any leftover cooked
Carrot	vegetables
Onions	Salt
Celery	Pepper

Cut fat off meat bones and dry out separately; strain into salvage tin. Put meat bones, bits of gristle and skin, all scraps, into saucepan; cover with cold water and add any gravy you are not planning to use in other ways. Let simmer gently for two or three hours. Strain into bowl, adding any scraps of meat from bones, etc., also add the browned pieces of fat from salvage. When cold, take off the fat, add raw vegetables, and cook gently until they are tender. Add leftover cooked vegetables, and when they are warmed through, season to taste.

Yankee Corn Chowder

2 slices bacon	1 cup diced cooked
2 tablespoons chopped onion	potatoes
2 tablespoons chopped green pepper	1½ cups cream-style corn
	2 cups milk
	½ teaspoon salt

Brown bacon in large pan; remove from pan; drain and crumble. Saute onion and green pepper in bacon fat until tender; add potatoes, corn, milk and salt. Heat thoroughly. Sprinkle chowder with crumbled bacon. Serve with crackers. Serves 4 to 6.

SALADS

SALADS were once confined to a few green herbs, but today they cover a wide range (as this section of the book testifies). They are an especially valuable part of the diet for the minerals and vitamins carried by the green leaves, roots, fruits and nuts so freely used as components.

For their enjoyment, the best materials are, however, necessary. Neither the appetizing appearance nor the food value of any combination is proof against the havoc that can be wrought by poor dressing.

Refreshing and wholesome, a salad is welcome at every table. "The poetry of comestibles," it's been called, and more than one sage has philosophized on its virtues.

Of course, that sage of the Bumstead family, Dagwood, would never be content with mere philosophizing. He'd have a try at making a new salad. His best remembered attempt at salad-making happened while he was home with a cold.

Alexander and Daisy were watching him add the finishing touches to a strange mixture. Blondie was outside in the garden.

Suddenly the still of the neighborhood was broken as Alexander and Daisy raced madly out the house, Alexander shouting, "Run, Mama, Run, here comes Daddy with the salad he just made!"

Dagwood appeared in the doorway, a large wooden bowl in his arms. "It's a little strong but good," he murmured.

Blondie, who came running to see what the trouble was, took a tiny sniff of the bowl's contents and turned away in a hurry. "You used ammonia instead of vinegar!" she admonished. Dagwood stood holding the bowl too overcome by the fumes to make an immediate reply.

"Well, it might be used in salads," he finally sheepishly blurted out, "nearly everything else is."

Tropic Salad

Sliced bananas	Shredded pineapple
Sliced oranges	Sliced pears
Sliced Brazilian nut meats	Grated cocoanut
Sliced peaches	Whipped and sweetened
Chopped dates	cream

Into a large salad dish put a layer of sliced bananas, a layer of oranges, a layer of nut meats, a layer of peaches, a layer of dates, then another layer of the nuts, a layer of pineapple, and a layer of pears. Sprinkle with the cocoanut, decorate with a few slices of nuts and small pieces of peaches, and serve with the cream.

Artichoke Salad

6 cooked or canned arti-	French dressing
choke bottoms	Peeled and sliced tomatoes
1 green pepper	Chopped chives
1 head celery	2 hard-cooked eggs
1 garlic clove	Salt and pepper to taste

Peel and crush the clove of garlic and add to the French dressing with the yolks of eggs rubbed through a sieve. Cut the artichoke bottoms, the celery and green pepper into fine strips, and mix them with the dressing. Turn into a flat salad dish, cover with the sliced tomatoes, sprinkle with salt and pepper, and decorate with chopped chives.

Cold sliced boiled Jerusalem artichokes may be served with French dressing seasoned with garlic or onion.

Another Method.—Boil eight fresh artichokes; separate the "fonds" from the leaves, and cut them into small pieces. Place them in a salad bowl with an equal amount of cooked asparagus tips. Chop one-half cupful of salted almonds, pound with them the strained juice of two lemons, add salt and pepper to taste, and one-half pint of cream. Pour over the salad and serve.

Or cut four artichoke bottoms in two-inch lengths and mix with one-half pound of shredded endive. Toss in a French dressing seasoned highly with paprika, and serve garnished with slices of hard-cooked eggs and sliced olives.

Asparagus Salad

Asparagus	½ teaspoonful salt
Lettuce leaves	¼ teaspoonful white
Hard-cooked eggs	pepper
Cheese wafers	½ teaspoonful grated
3 tablespoonfuls olive oil	onion
1 tablespoonful vinegar	½ teaspoonful grated
½ tablespoonful lemon-juice	horseradish

Remove the tough ends of asparagus, and, after washing the stalks, cook them in boiling salted water until tender; drain, and when cool, lay on a bed of crisp lettuce leaves and cover with the sauce. Garnish with the hard-cooked eggs cut in slices, and serve with cheese wafers. Mix the olive oil with the vinegar and lemon-juice; add the salt, pepper, onion, and horseradish; let stand for one hour, then strain out the onion and horseradish, and you have the appropriate dressing.

Asparagus and Ham Salad

1 bundle cooked asparagus	Mayonnaise dressing
¼ lb. cooked lean ham	Mashed potatoes
2 hard-cooked eggs	Radishes
1 cucumber	Chopped onion tops

Cut the ham, cucumber, and eggs into small strips. Remove the heads from the asparagus and cut the stalks into small lengths. Mix the eggs, ham, cucumber, and asparagus together and place them in a salad bowl and cover with mayonnaise dressing sprinkled with green onion tops.

Put the potatoes into a forcing bag with large star tube and force them out around the edge of the dish. Then stick in the potatoes some tips of asparagus and slices of red radishes, sprinkle over with a little chopped ham, and serve very cold.

Another Method.—Mix the tender parts of some cooked asparagus with minced ham sauce. Place in the salad dish and serve garnished with sprigs of cooked cauliflower and finely chopped green peppers.

Avocado and Grapefruit Salad

1 avocado pear	1 chopped shallot
½ pint (1 cupful) grape-	1 teaspoonful salt
fruit pulp	1 teaspoonful sugar
1 chopped green pepper	3 tablespoonfuls vinegar
½ pint (1 cup) chopped	6 tablespoonfuls olive oil
crisp celery	

Peel the pear with a silver knife and cut it into dice. Put the pieces in a salad bowl, and mix with the grapefruit pulp and juice. Put the shallot into a small bowl, add the salt, sugar, vinegar and oil. Stir and mix well. Then add the pepper. Pour it over the pear and grapefruit, then mix and chill. At serving time, add the celery, mixing it in gently.

Another Method.—Peel and cut an avocado pear, and then toss lightly with some grapefruit pulp and a few skinned and seeded grapes, using two silver forks for the purpose. Chill the ingredients, and at serving time arrange on a bed of white, crisp lettuce leaves; then over all pour a fruit mayonnaise made as follows: Beat up two yolks of eggs with two tablespoonfuls of sifted sugar, add slowly two tablespoonfuls of lemon-juice, stirring all the time, then gradually add two tablespoonfuls of sherry wine. Beat thoroughly with an egg-beater. Serve very cold. Or put an avocado pear through a potato ricer, add onion-juice to taste, and fill into skinned tomato shells. Garnish with slices of hard-cooked egg and serve on lettuce nests with mayonnaise dressing.

Banana and Date Salad

Bananas	French dressing
Stoned and sliced dates	Crisp white lettuce leaves
Shredded celery	Cress or parsley
Broken pecan nut meats	

Take a strip from the top of each banana and dice the contents. Add to the banana equal quantities of dates, celery, and nut meats, and mix with French dressing made with lemon-juice. Fill the banana-skin boats with the salad and serve on lettuce leaves garnished with cress or parsley.

Or cut peeled bananas into four strips, chop some peanuts fine, and roll the bananas in the chopped nuts. When ready to serve, put a crisp lettuce leaf on a plate with one-half table-spoonful of green mayonnaise heaped on it. Lay a strip of banana on either side of the leaf and serve, passing a dish of mayonnaise dressing at the same time.

Beet and Onion Salad

1 large cooked Spanish onion	1 teaspoonful chopped parsley
1 large cooked beet	Salt and pepper to taste
1 teaspoonful chopped tarragon	4 tablespoonfuls olive oil
	2 tablespoonfuls vinegar

Slice the onion, add the beet chopped and the seasonings, oil, and vinegar. Mix well and serve with cold roast beef.

A little grated horseradish is an improvement to this salad if the flavor is liked.

Bermuda Salad

6 small sliced Bermuda onions	1 small cucumber
2 pints (4 cups) cooked stringbeans	8 tablespoonfuls olive oil
1 bunch watercress	2 tablespoonfuls vinegar
1 lettuce	½ teaspoonful salt
1 bunch radishes	¼ teaspoonful pepper
	French dressing

Cut the radishes into roses and dice the cucumber. Cut the beans lengthwise, cover them with a little French dressing, and leave them in a cool place for two hours. Beat up the oil and vinegar together and season with the salt and pepper.

Place the lettuce and cress in a salad dish, add the onions, surround with the beans; add the cucumber to the dressing and pour over the salad. Decorate with the radish roses and serve very cold.

Blue Bird Salad

1 orange	1 apple
½ pint (1 cup) chopped pineapple	½ gill (¼ cup) olive oil
½ grapefruit	1 lemon
1 banana	1 tablespoonful sugar
½ pint (1 cup) white grapes	1 teaspoonful salt
	½ teaspoonful paprika
½ pint (1 cup) shredded celery	Boiled raisins
	Mayonnaise dressing

Cut the grapes in half and remove the seeds; free the grapefruit and orange pulp from the containing membrane, and cut the apple and banana into dice. Mix the fruit with the celery.

Mix the sugar, salt, and paprika together; add one tablespoonful of the oil; stir well, then gradually add the rest of the oil, beating constantly. Now add the strained juice of the lemon, pour over the fruits, and allow to stand for one hour. Drain, arrange on crisp lettuce leaves, decorate with one-half cupful of boiled raisins, and serve with mayonnaise.

Cabbage and Celery Salad

1 head crisp celery	1 cabbage
Salt and red pepper	1 teaspoonful mustard
1 oz. (2 tablespoonfuls) butter	2 egg-yolks
1 teaspoonful flour	4 tablespoonfuls cream
1½ gills (¾ cup) cider vinegar	3 tablespoonfuls whipped cream
	1 tablespoonful sugar

Chop the cabbage and the celery, mix well, and sprinkle

with one teaspoonful of salt. Blend the butter and flour together in the upper pan of a double boiler, add the mustard, sugar, vinegar, yolks of eggs, and the single cream. Cook, stirring constantly until smooth and thick. Season with red pepper, pour over the cabbage and celery, and stand away to cool. At serving time add the whipped cream.

Shredded red cabbage and finely cut celery seasoned with onion-juice and served with French dressing make an attractive salad.

Cabbage salad as an accompaniment to a fish course is sometimes served in cups of lemon, tomato, or cooked beets with a little mayonnaise dressing on the top.

A *Cooked Salad.*—Mix together two cupfuls of chopped cabbage, two chopped apples, and one-half cupful of chopped black walnut meats, and sprinkle over with a little salt. Cover with the following dressing: Mix together one-half tablespoonful each of salt and mustard, one tablespoonful of sugar, two tablespoonfuls of butter, one beaten egg, and one cupful of cream. Cook in a double boiler, adding one-third cupful of vinegar, and stir until it thickens, but do not allow to boil.

Cabbage Salad in Cabbage Shell

1 cabbage	½ teaspoonful black
4 cucumbers	pepper
5 onions	¼ teaspoonful paprika
1 pint (2 cups) cooked	10 pimientoes (canned
beans	red peppers)
1 bunch celery	Mayonnaise dressing
1 tablespoonful salt	Chopped parsley

Select a crisp head of cabbage, not too large. Remove the outer leaves, and take out the heart of the cabbage, leaving a thin shell. Chop the cabbage, removed, very fine; add the seasonings and the beans. Chop the cucumbers, celery, pimientoes, and onions, and add them to the cabbage. Mix with the mayonnaise dressing and turn into the cabbage shell. Decorate with chopped parsley and serve very cold.

Carrot Salad

1½ pints (3 cups) cooked diced carrots
½ pint (1 cup) cooked asparagus tips
½ pint (1 cup) cooked green peas
Watercress or lettuce
Chopped chives or parsley

1 egg
1 tablespoonful butter
1 teaspoonful salt
½ teaspoonful dry mustard
2 tablespoonfuls sugar
1½ gills (¾ cup) vinegar
2 tablespoonfuls cream

Mix the carrots with the asparagus tips and a little chopped parsley and one-half of the dressing. At serving time serve the salad on the watercress or lettuce, decorate with the peas in little heaps, and pour over the remainder of the dressing.

For the dressing: Beat the butter and sugar to a cream in a small saucepan, add the egg beaten, salt, mustard, and vinegar, and stir over the fire until thick. Cool and add the cream.

Cauliflower and Beet Salad

1 large cauliflower
1 tablespoonful salt

Pickled beets
Cream salad dressing

Wash the cauliflower and boil it for thirty minutes in boiling water in which the salt has been dissolved. Drain, and

when cold, divide it into small branches. Arrange these in the center of a salad dish and garnish the edge with the beets cut in strips. Pour over cream salad dressing and serve at once.

Another Method.—Place a cold boiled cauliflower on ice until ready to serve; then break into branches and set on crisp lettuce leaves. Garnish with pimientoes and cover with mayonnaise dressing.

Cantaloupe Salad

Cantaloupes	Lettuce leaves
French dressing	Paprika

Quarter the cantaloupes, remove the seeds and the outer rinds. Place a quarter on lettuce leaves on each salad plate, and serve with French dressing made with lime- or lemon-juice.

Another Method.—Cut the pulp of cantaloupes into cubes, season lightly with salt and paprika, and serve on shredded endive with mayonnaise dressing to which whipped cream or cream cheese is added.

Casaba or Honeydew Melon Salad

1 melon	White cream cheese
Seeded white grapes	French or mayonnaise
Crisp lettuce leaves	dressing

Cut a Casaba melon into balls with a potato cutter. Peel and seed an equal quantity of white grapes, mix them with the melon balls, and put into nests of lettuce leaves, then put the cheese through a ricer over each nest. Serve with French or mayonnaise dressing.

Calf's Brain Salad

1 set calf's brains	3 stalks celery
½ pint (1 cup) chopped nut meats	Mayonnaise or boiled dressing
1 small bottle stuffed olives	Parsley

Scald the brains with boiling water to cleanse them. Boil them until tender in fresh, cold; salted water, being careful to remove from the water while yet firm. Cut in small pieces and mix with the nut meats, the olives cut in halves, and the celery cut in small pieces. Chill, and serve mixed with mayonnaise or boiled dressing, and garnish with sprigs of parsley.

Cheese Salad

4 heads of lettuce	1 teaspoonful chopped parsley
½ cucumber	
6 spring onions	1 tablespoonful grated Parmesan cheese
Salt and paprika	
2 egg-yolks	Salad oil
2 tablespoonfuls tarragon vinegar	2 tablespoonfuls cream
	Cheese cubes

Cut the head of lettuce into quarters and slice the onions and cucumber. Put these in layers in a salad bowl, sprinkling a little salt and paprika between each layer. Mix the yolks of eggs smooth with the tarragon vinegar, add the chopped parsley, grated Parmesan cheese, cream, and enough salad oil to make a thin sauce. Pour this dressing over the salad and decorate with the cubes of cheese.

Another Method.—Cut into small pieces one-half pound of cheese and a green sweet pepper. Mix two tablespoonfuls of peanut butter with one cupful of mayonnaise dressing, and add the cheese and pepper. Chill and serve with toasted crackers.

Cherry and Cream Cheese Salad

White or red canned cherries	Chopped English walnut meats
Cream cheese	Lettuce leaves or endive
	French dressing

Remove the stones from large canned red or white cherries and fill with a mixture of cream cheese and chopped nut meats. Serve on endive or crisp lettuce leaves with French dressing.

Another Method.—Stone one pint of ripe cherries, drain well, and mix with one peeled and diced cucumber and one-half cupful of blanched and chopped almonds. Arrange on lettuce leaves and serve covered with the following dressing: Mix four tablespoonfuls of cherry juice with two tablespoonfuls of lemon-juice, four tablespoonfuls of sugar, and two drops of almond extract. Serve very cold.

Chestnut and Celery Salad

1 lb. chestnuts	Vinegar
1 head celery	Salt and pepper
1 crisp lettuce	1 onion
1 tomato, skinned	1 clove
Mayonnaise dressing	Herbs
Chopped parsley	Boiling stock
Peanut or olive oil	

Shell and slit the chestnuts, boil them for ten minutes in water, drain off the water, and peel them carefully; now put them in a stewpan, cover with boiling stock, add a small bouquet of herbs and the onion stuck with the clove, and boil until tender. When done, drain and let cool; wash the celery

and trim it, then shred it fine; wash and shred the lettuce, cut the chestnuts into slices and put them into a salad bowl with the celery, season with enough mayonnaise sauce to dress the salad, pile up rather high, and surround it with finely shredded lettuce to form a border; cut the tomato into slices, season with oil, vinegar, salt, and pepper, and place this in the center, or in groups around the chestnuts and celery; sprinkle with chopped parsley and serve.

Other nuts may be used in the same way.

Chicken Salad No. 1

1 cooked chicken	Chopped aspic jelly
Endive	Chopped parsley
Lettuce	Salt and paprika
6 hard-cooked eggs	Whipped cream sauce

Take the best white part of the chicken and cut the meat into little squares, then place the pieces in a basin and mix well with the sauce. Line a salad bowl with pieces of endive and lettuce, then turn in the chicken mixture, cut the hard-cooked eggs in halves and place them around the salad, place a tablespoonful of chopped aspic jelly between each egg, and sprinkle the eggs with salt and paprika to taste and a little chopped parsley.

To make the whipped cream sauce: Chop four hard-cooked eggs, rub them through a wire sieve into a basin, add two dessertspoonfuls of olive oil, two dessertspoonfuls of tarragon vinegar, salt, pepper, and mustard to taste; one-half tablespoonful of capers and one teaspoonful of chopped parsley; mix well with a wooden spoon, then add one cupful of whipped cream.

Chicken Salad No. 2

1 cold cooked chicken	1 teaspoonful made
Chopped celery	mustard
2 hard-cooked eggs	2 teaspoonfuls sugar
1 raw egg	3 teaspoonfuls olive oil
½ teaspoonful white	½ gill(½ teacup) vinegar
pepper	Lettuce
	1 teaspoonful salt

Chop the white meat of a cold broiled or roasted chicken; add three-fourths of the same amount of celery, and set aside in a cool place. Rub the yolks of the hard-cooked eggs through a sieve, add the salt, pepper, sugar, mustard, and oil. Beat up the raw egg, beat it into the dressing, and gradually add the vinegar, whipping the dressing all the time. Sprinkle a little salt over the chicken and celery, add the dressing, and toss and mix with a silver fork. Serve in a lettuce-lined salad bowl, decorated with the whites of the hard-cooked eggs cut into rings or flowers.

One cupful of chopped English walnut meats makes a nice addition to chicken salad.

This salad is delicious served in green pepper cups, with nut or cream cheese sandwiches cut in long thin strips.

Chicory Salad

Chicory	Garlic or onion-juice
French dressing	

Wash the chicory and put it into cold water for a few minutes; then drain well. Dress with French dressing seasoned with onion-juice, or rub the inside of the salad bowl with a piece of garlic.

Or, if a heartier salad is desired, grate over the chicory some Roquefort cheese and mix one tablespoonful of chili sauce with the dressing before pouring over the salad.

Chiffonade Salad

Lettuce or endive
½ pint (1 cup) shredded celery
¼ pint (½ cup) cooked beans
¼ pint (½ cup) cooked beets, chopped
1 chopped onion
2 tablespoonfuls chopped parsley
1 chopped green pepper
2 skinned and chopped tomatoes

1 grapefruit
½ teaspoonful salt
¼ teaspoonful pepper
¼ teaspoonful onion-juice
1 tablespoonful vinegar
1 tablespoonful lemon-juice
1 chopped hard-cooked egg
1 teaspoonful chopped chives
1 teaspoonful chopped pimientoes
6 tablespoonfuls olive oil

Mix the shredded celery, beans, beets, onion, parsley, green pepper, tomatoes, and grapefruit pulp well together and arrange on lettuce or endive. Stir together the salt, pepper, onion-juice, vinegar, lemon-juice, egg, chives, pimientoes, and gradually add the olive oil. When well blended, pour over the salad and serve.

Cream Cheese and Pimiento Salad

Cream cheese
Pimientoes
Crisp lettuce leaves

French or mayonnaise dressing
Celery

Drain the pimientoes, wipe and chop them, and add sufficient to cream cheese to give a decided flavor. Roll into balls the size of a walnut, and place four on lettuce leaves on individual plates. Pour over either French dressing or thin mayonnaise dressing. Serve with crisp celery.

This mixture is also excellent for sandwiches.

Cream Cheese and Pineapple Salad

2 cream cheeses

2 cans pineapple

1 lettuce

1 orange

¼ lb. (½ cup) sugar

Boil the strained juice of the orange, sugar, and pineapple juice together for five minutes and chill. On a leaf of lettuce put one slice of pineapple. Put the cheese through a potato ricer, covering the pineapple, then pour over a little of the chilled syrup.

Cole-Slaw

Cabbage

½ pint (1 cup) thick sour cream

1 gill (½ cup) vinegar

1 gill (½ cup) sugar

½ teaspoonful salt

⅛ teaspoonful white pepper

Chop fine one-fourth of a head of cabbage and divide into eight small salad dishes. Beat up the cream, add gradually and alternately the vinegar and sugar, and then add the salt and pepper. Put two tablespoonfuls of this dressing upon the top of each portion and set in a cool place for fifteen minutes before serving. This salad is a "must" to Dagwood with hamburger steak.

Corn, Nut and Celery Salad

1 pint (2 cups) cooked
grated corn
½ pint (1 cup) chopped
English walnut meats

½ pint (1 cup) chopped
celery
Pepper and salt
Chopped onion

Mix the corn with the nuts and the celery, and add the seasonings. Serve in crisp lettuce.

Boiled Salad Dressing

2 eggs
1 oz. (2 tablespoonfuls)
butter
1 gill (½ cup) hot vinegar
½ pint (1 cup) scalded
milk

1 teaspoonful salt
1 teaspoonful sugar
1 teaspoonful mustard
¼ teaspoonful white
pepper

To prepare, mix the seasonings with the beaten yolks of eggs and stir until smooth. Melt the butter in the vinegar and add it slowly to the eggs in the upper pan of a double boiler. Stir in the milk gradually and cook until thickened, but do not allow to boil. Let cool a little, then stir in the whites of eggs stiffly beaten. Thin with a little cream, either sweet or sour, when ready to use. Keep in a cool place and do not add to a salad until a few minutes before it is to be served. Some like it better without the mustard.

Crab-Meat Salad

1 quart (4 cups) crab meat
1 pint (2 cups) shredded
lettuce or celery
2 tablespoonfuls olive oil
4 tablespoonfuls vinegar

Salt and pepper to taste
Mayonnaise dressing
2 chopped hard-cooked
eggs
Chopped parsley

Mix the crab meat with the lettuce or celery, olive oil, vinegar, and seasonings. Divide into salad dishes, decorate with the eggs and parsley, and serve with the mayonnaise dressing.

Another Method.—Mix together two cupfuls of crab meat, one-third cupful of cooked asparagus tips, one chopped pickled walnut, and two shredded lettuces; add salt, pepper, and paprika to taste, and mix with mayonnaise dressing. Put on a salad plate and garnish with slices of hard-cooked egg and strips of green and red peppers.

Dandelion Salad

Dandelion leaves	Watercress
Crisp lettuce	Hard-cooked eggs
French dressing	

Wash and dry tender leaves of young dandelions, and mix them with double the quantity of shredded lettuce. Mix with the French dressing and serve decorated with watercress and chopped hard-cooked eggs.

Chopped spring onions or chopped chives are excellent with dandelions and French dressing.

Egg and Lobster Salad

Hard-cooked eggs	French dressing
1 boiled lobster	Cream cheese
Celery	Whipped cream
Cucumber	Strips of toast
Mayonnaise dressing	Salt and pepper
Crisp lettuce	

Cook a number of eggs—one to each person, remove the shells, cut a small piece from the top and a slice from the bottom of each—the latter to make them stand; remove the yolks, fill the whites with lobster, celery, and cucumber, all cut fine, and mixed with the mayonnaise dressing. Serve one of these to each person upon individual salad plates of lettuce garnished with the yolks highly seasoned and made into tiny balls. Sprinkle over with French dressing, and serve with snow-balls made of cream cheese and whipped cream, mashed smooth, and long strips of toast.

Canned lobster may be used.

Dandelion and Oyster Salad

1 pint (2 cups) undeveloped dandelion buds	Salt
	Tabasco sauce
1 pint (2 cups) oysters	Lemon-juice
French dressing	Dandelion leaves

Mix the dandelion leaves with French dressing and line a salad bowl with them. Scald the oysters, drain, and sprinkle them with salt, tabasco, and lemon-juice, and set them in a cool place for two hours. Drain them and cut them in halves or quarters, and mix them with the dandelion buds. Serve in the prepared salad bowl.

Cooked lobster, shrimps, or scallops may be substituted for the oysters.

Egg Salad

1 envelope unflavored gelatin	2 tablespoons chopped green pepper
¼ cup cold water	2 tablespoons pickle relish
4 hard cooked eggs, sliced or diced	1 tablespoon chopped pimiento
½ cup chopped celery	1 tablespoon lemon juice
1 cup mayonnaise	¾ teaspoonful salt

Soften gelatin in cold water, place bowl over boiling water and stir until gelatin is dissolved; cool and beat into mayonnaise. Add other ingredients and mix thoroughly. Turn into loaf pan that has been rinsed in cold water and chill. When firm, unmold, and slice very thin. Arrange slice of egg salad on lettuce and garnish with slices of tomato, cucumber or radish roses.

Endive Salad

2 heads endive	2 tablespoonfuls honey
1 chopped shallot	2 tablespoonfuls vinegar
3 tablespoonfuls olive oil	Salt and pepper to taste

Remove the outer leaves of the endive; wash the inner ones; drain and dry and place in a salad bowl; then sprinkle over the olive oil mixed with the shallot. Let stand in a cool place until ready to serve, and just before sending to table pour over the salad the honey, vinegar, and seasonings mixed together.

If liked, finely shredded celery or sprigs of watercress may be mixed with this salad.

Another Method.—Cover the endive with ice water, drain, and shake dry, and serve with French dressing. Garnish with chopped chives and chopped nuts, or with diced tomatoes and grated Parmesan cheese.

Church–Supper Salad

1 cooked chicken	1 lb. English walnut
1 bunch celery	meats
1 orange	6 sweet pickles
1 can sliced pineapple	1 can peas
2½ dozen hard-cooked	Salt, pepper, and paprika
eggs	to taste
16 candied cherries	Boiled salad dressing

This recipe serves twenty-five persons.

Chop the chicken, celery, orange, nut meats, eggs, pickles, and drained pineapple, then add the drained peas and seasonings. Mix with the boiled salad dressing and serve on lettuce leaves. Place the cherries on the top.

Fish Salad No. 1

Sliced cucumbers	Cold cooked lobster or
Mayonnaise dressing	salmon

Take some scallop shells, allowing one for each person, and arrange some thinly sliced cucumber all around the shells by folding the slices in halves so as not to break; leave a small space in the center, then take a few neat pieces of salmon or lobster, or any preferred fish, and fill up this space. Cover with mayonnaise dressing, and serve on a silver dish.

Another Method.—Let cubes of cooked fish roe, mixed with paprika, oil, vinegar, salt, pepper, and lemon-juice, stand in a cool place until ready to serve. Drain and add an equal quantity of peeled and diced cucumber, also one tablespoonful of chopped parsley, and top with mayonnaise to which one-half cupful of whipped cream has been added. Serve on watercress or lettuce.

Fish Salad No. 2

1 lettuce	Salt and pepper
1 endive	1 lb. cooked fish
1 cucumber	Mayonnaise dressing
1 cooked or canned beet	½ pint (1 cup) whipped
2 tablespoonfuls white	cream
vinegar	2 tablespoonfuls freshly
2 tablespoonfuls olive oil	grated horseradish
1 teaspoonful mustard	2 tablespoonfuls chopped
	red or green peppers

Pick the lettuce and endive into neat pieces, cut the cucumber and beet into dice and turn into a basin, add the vinegar, oil, mustard, salt, and pepper; mix well, and place in a salad bowl or silver dish; then make a hole in the center, place in the fish picked into neat pieces, and pour over mayonnaise dressing; mix well, add one-fourth teaspoonful of salt to the whipped cream, place this on top with a bag and tube, and decorate with the horseradish and peppers.

Frogs' Legs Salad

2 dozen large frogs' legs	3 ozs. (¾ cup) blanched
½ pint (1 cup) diced celery or cucumbers	and shredded almonds
2 tablespoonfuls chopped pimientoes	Nasturtium leaves and blossoms (or cress)
A few pecan nut meats	Mild mayonnaise or French dressing

Cook the frogs' legs in boiling salted water until tender, then remove the meat from the bones and cut it into cubes. Mix it with the celery or cucumber, the pimientoes, almonds, and pecan nut meats. Place in nests of nasturtium leaves, decorate with the blossoms, and serve with the dressing.

Frozen Cheese Salad

1 lb. cheese
¼ lb. pecan nut meats
1 can pimientoes
½ pint (1 cup) chopped
    cucumber pickles
Salted wafers

1 pint (2 cups) whipping
    cream
Salt and red pepper to
    taste
Crisp lettuce leaves
Mayonnaise dressing

Put the cheese and nuts through a food-chopper, add the pimientoes cut in small strips, the pickles and seasonings, and fold in the whipped cream. Divide into round molds lined with paper, cover, and pack in ice and salt for three hours. Slice into rounds, place one on a lettuce leaf for each person, top with a spoonful of the mayonnaise dressing, and serve with the wafers.

Fruit Salads

There is an infinite variety of these in which every kind of fresh, canned or frozen fruit may be featured. A number of recipes are grouped here. Others will be found under individual headings. (See the index in the front of the book.)

No. 1.—Mix equal quantities of diced apples, bananas, celery, and pineapple with mayonnaise dressing. Serve in a scooped-out pineapple, decorated with squares of lemon jelly. The pineapple may be sliced at the side and scooped out instead of cutting a slice from the top.

No. 2.—Drain twelve canned artichoke bottoms, marinate with French dressing, cover, and let stand in a cold place until thoroughly chilled. Pile up with grapefruit and orange pulp, which has also been drained and marinated. Arrange in nests of crisp lettuce leaves, pour over French dressing.

No. 3.—Cut in dice twelve strawberries, one apple, one orange, one apricot, one banana, and four slices of canned pineapple. Mix with one-half cupful of sherry wine and set in a cool place for one hour. Serve on individual salad plates, covered with whipped and sweetened cream, and decorated with strips of French endive and halves of ripe strawberries.

No. 4.—Cut thirty marshmallows in small pieces, add one-fourth pound of broken pecan nut meats, one pound of white grapes, seeded and cut in halves, and one can of pineapple, drained and diced.

Mix the yolks of four eggs with one-half teaspoonful of salt, one-fourth of a teaspoonful of mustard, and the strained juice of one lemon. Bring to boiling-point and cool. Pour over the salad, then add two cupfuls of whipped cream. Allow to stand over night in a cool place and serve on crisp lettuce leaves.

No. 5.—Mix one cupful of grapefruit pulp with one cupful of diced canned apricots and one cupful of seeded grapes. Beat the yolks of four eggs in the upper pan of a double boiler, add four tablespoonfuls of vinegar, one-fourth teaspoonful of mustard, and one-fourth cupful of butter; cook until thick, take from the fire, and add salt and pepper to taste. Add two tablespoonfuls of powdered gelatine dissolved in one-half cupful of boiling water; then cool and add one cupful of cream and the fruit. Pour into a mold, cover, and pack in ice and salt for three hours. Turn out and serve with mayonnaise dressing.

No. 6.—Wash three ripe persimmons, but do not skin, as their skins are nutritious and add to the taste, then slice in one-fourth inch slices, add three-fourths pound of seeded grapes cut in halves. Serve on lettuce hearts, with French dressing poured over. Decorate with chopped nut meats.

No. 7.—Cut up one box of marshmallows, add three diced bananas, one cupful of chopped English walnut meats, one can of grated pineapple, and three crackers rolled fine. Make a syrup of one-half cupful of sugar and one-half cupful of vinegar; when cool, add one-half cupful of whipped cream and pour over the salad.

No. 8.—Mix one-half cupful of blanched and chopped almonds with four medium-sized peeled and diced apples, two diced bananas, the pulp of two oranges, one cupful of stoned white cherries, one cupful of peeled and seeded grapes, and one-half cupful of stoned and chopped dates. Beat up the yolks of two eggs in a small saucepan, add five tablespoonfuls of vinegar, two tablespoonfuls of water or fruit-juice, one tablespoonful of sugar, and one-fourth teaspoonful of salt. Cook slowly over hot water until thick, stirring constantly, but do not boil. Add one teaspoonful of butter, beat well, and set aside to cool. When cold, add the stiffly beaten whites of the eggs and one-third pint of double cream whipped very stiff. Fold the fruit into the dressing and serve on lettuce leaves.

No. 9.—Rub a salad bowl with lemon slices and sprinkle in some powdered sugar. Put in a layer of ripe raspberries, sprinkle with sugar, and so on until the dish is full. Over it pour a wineglassful of sherry wine and chill before serving. Or have liquid wine jelly, and just as it is about to harden pour over the raspberries.

No. 10.—Arrange a border of crisp white endive leaves around a salad dish. Mix together two sliced bananas, one cupful of fresh or preserved stoned cherries, the pulp of two grapefruit, and one cupful of pineapple cut into cubes. Mix one cupful of mayonnaise sauce with one cupful of whipped cream, season to taste with salt, pepper, paprika, and mushroom catchup, and serve with the salad.

No. 11.—Peel and chop three apples, dice enough pineapple to make one cupful, mix with one diced banana and one cupful of orange- and lemon-juice mixed, then add one-half cupful of blanched and shredded almonds, and stand on ice. Beat the yolks of four eggs in a saucepan, add one cupful of vinegar, and cook until it thickens; add one tablespoonful of sugar, salt, pepper, and paprika to taste. When cold, add one cupful of whipped cream and pour over the fruit. Serve in orange or lemon shells, garnish with whipped cream and strips of angelica.

No. 12.—Dice four bananas, and sprinkle over with lemon-juice; add the unbroken sections of four mandarin oranges, a small shredded pineapple, and one cupful of seeded and skinned white grapes. Chill and serve with the following dressing: Put into a small saucepan one cupful of sugar and one-half cupful of water and boil for five minutes; then pour this syrup over the well-beaten yolks of three eggs, stirring all the time. Cook in the upper pan of a double boiler until it thickens, then chill and add the strained juice of two lemons.

Fruit salads may be served for the middle course of a dinner, or as a sweet, or as the principal dish of a simple luncheon. They should be served in dainty cups or glasses.

Fruit Salad a la Russe

Ripe strawberries	Powdered sugar
Raspberries or loganberries	Brandy
Red and white currants	Lemon jelly
Stoned cherries	Grapes
Oranges	Pastry fingers
Bananas	

Mix equal quantities of strawberries, raspberries, currants, grapes, and cherries, add two or three oranges diced, two or three bananas cut up small, and turn into a salad bowl. Sprinkle over with powdered sugar and brandy to taste. Whip up some liquid lemon jelly to a stiff froth, pile in rough heaps on the top of the fruit, and chill before serving.

Pass small pastry fingers with this salad.

Herring Salad

3 pickled herrings
4 cold boiled potatoes
2 tart apples
1 tablespoonful celery
seed
1 tablespoonful tarragon
vinegar
1 teaspoonful salt

½ teaspoonful paprika
7 tablespoonfuls olive oil
1 tablespoonful lemon-
juice
2 tablespoonfuls malt
vinegar
1 teaspoonful French
mustard
Watercress or endive

Skin and cut the herrings into small pieces; slice the potatoes and the apples, and mix them together with the celery seed and tarragon vinegar; set in a cool place until wanted. Put the salt and pepper into a bowl, add the oil, and stir and rub until the salt is dissolved; then add the lemon-juice and malt vinegar; mix well, and add the French mustard. Line a salad bowl with watercress or endive, place in the fish and vegetables, pour over the dressing, and serve.

Chopped hard-cooked eggs and cooked beets and small pickles may be added to this salad if liked.

Frozen Tomato Salad

6 ripe tomatoes	½ teaspoonful sugar
2 tablespoonfuls powdered gelatine	2 tablespoonfuls lemon-juice
½ pint (1 cup) boiling water	Lettuce leaves
1 teaspoonful salt	Mayonnaise dressing
½ teaspoonful paprika	French dressing

Peel the tomatoes, then chop them and rub through a sieve. Add the gelatine dissolved in the boiling water and the seasonings. Beat until it begins to thicken, then pour into a wet ring mold. Pack in equal parts of rock salt and crushed ice for four hours. Turn out and fill the center with lettuce dipped in French dressing and serve with mayonnaise dressing.

Ginger Ale Salad

1½ ozs. (4½ tablespoonfuls) powdered gelatine	2 tablespoonfuls lemon-juice
6 ozs. (¾ cup) sugar	Lettuce leaves
1½ pints (3 cups) ginger ale	Mayonnaise or French dressing
½ pint (1 cup) water	Chopped nut meats

Mix the sugar and gelatine and dissolve them in the water over the fire; add the lemon-juice and ginger ale, divide into small wet molds, and set in a cool place to chill. Turn out on heart leaves of lettuce, sprinkle over with finely chopped nut meats, and serve with French or mayonnaise dressing.

If liked, the jelly may be poured into a flat, wet tin, and when firm, cut into squares.

Green Dressing Salad

Aspic or lemon jelly	Broken English walnut meats
Canned or cold cooked peas	Watercress
Green mayonnaise dressing	Cut lemons
Whipped cream	

Mold the jelly in small individual charlotte russe molds, and turn out at serving time on to individual salad plates. Fill with the peas and garnish with the watercress and fancy cut lemons. Serve with green mayonnaise dressing to which has been added a little whipped cream and walnut meats. The jelly may be molded in cups, and the centers removed with a warm spoon.

Horseradish and Celery Salad

½ oz. (1½ tablespoonfuls) powdered gelatine
1 pint (2 cups) boiling water
2 lemons
4 ozs. (½ cup) sugar
1 tablespoonful freshly grated horseradish

Few drops green color
½ pint (1 cup) finely chopped celery
1 gill (½ cup) chopped nut meats
Lettuce leaves
Mayonnaise dressing

Dissolve the gelatine in the water, add the strained juice of the lemons, the sugar, horseradish, and green color. Pour this over the celery and the nut meats and pour into a wet mold. Turn out when firm on to lettuce leaves and serve with mayonnaise dressing.

Jellied Chicken and Rice Salad

1 oz. (3 tablespoonfuls) powdered gelatine
3 cupfuls boiling water
Salt and pepper to taste
Celery salt and paprika to taste
2 tablespoonfuls chopped canned red peppers

1½ gills (¾ cup) cold boiled rice
½ pint (1 cup) diced cold cooked chicken
Endive
Mayonnaise dressing
1 gill (½ cup) chopped olives

Dissolve the gelatine in the water, add the red peppers and seasonings. Wet a square mold and scatter over the bottom some of the olives, rice, and chicken; now pour over this a layer of the gelatine and set on ice to stiffen; keep the rest of the gelatine where it is warm enough to prevent its hardening. When the first layer is firm, repeat the process; then put in the refrigerator until ready to serve. Turn out and cut into small squares and serve on endive with mayonnaise dressing.

Macédoine Salad

Cooked string or French
  beans
Cooked asparagus tops
Cooked carrots
Cooked turnips

Cooked green peas
Cooked lima or green
  beans
Cooked cauliflower
Mayonnaise dressing

The cauliflower should be broken into small pieces, and the carrots and turnips should be cut into dice-shaped pieces before cooking. Drain and dry all the vegetables, then mix them with a rich mayonnaise dressing to which some whipped cream has been added. Arrange all the vegetables carefully in a salad dish, and decorate with pieces of the various vegetables.

Prepared macédoine of vegetables, sold in bottles or tins, may be used for this salad; these require to be rinsed in water and drained before using.

Another Method:—Take a ring mold, butter it, and press into it three and one-half cupfuls of hot boiled rice, seasoned to taste with salt, pepper, and paprika and three tablespoonfuls of melted butter. When cold, turn out on to a salad dish and fill with a macédoine of vegetables mixed with French dressing.

Hot Vegetable Salad

¾ pint (1½ cups) shred-
  ded cooked string-beans
¾ pint (1½ cups) cooked
  or canned peas
¾ pint (1½ cups) cooked
  whole young carrots
¼ pint (½ cup) cooked
  shredded salsify
1 boiled lettuce, shredded
2 large tomatoes
2 slices onion

1 teaspoonful vinegar
1 teaspoonful meat extract
Salt and pepper to taste
2 sprigs parsley
1 bay-leaf
½ pint (1 cup) stock or
  water
1 teaspoonful chopped
  chutney
½ teaspoonful Worcester-
  shire sauce

Slice the tomatoes into a saucepan, add onion, vinegar, meat extract, salt and pepper to taste, parsley, bay-leaf, and stock or water; boil for twelve minutes, strain, and add the Worcestershire sauce and the chutney, the peas, beans, and lettuce. Mix and pile high in the center of a hot dish; now arrange the carrots around the edge, points upward, with the pieces of salsify between; set in the oven to get smoking hot, and serve at once.

Hot Slaw

1 cabbage	¼ teaspoonful pepper
Salt	⅛ teaspoonful red pepper
Butter	½ teaspoonful mustard
4 tablespoonfuls milk	1 beaten egg
1 tablespoonful vinegar	1 gill (½ cup) boiling
1 teaspoonful sugar	cream

Shred the cabbage very fine, measure it, and put it into an enameled saucepan; to every two cupfuls of it allow one-half cupful of boiling water and a teaspoonful of salt and cook until perfectly tender.

Add the milk and one tablespoonful of butter, and continue to cook until the cabbage is dry; then serve with the following sauce: Put the seasonings and vinegar into a pan, bring to boiling-point, add the egg, one teaspoonful of butter, and the boiling cream. Serve hot. This is a salad Dagwood likes with lamb stew.

Jellied Beet and Nut Salad

1 bunch boiled beets	½ oz. (1½ tablespoon-
¼ pint (½ cup) chopped	fuls) powdered gelatine
nut meats	½ pint (1 cup) hot water
½ pint (1 cup) heavy may-	or stock
onnaise dressing	Shredded lettuce or cab-
	bage

Chop the beets. Dissolve the gelatine in the water, then cool and mix with the mayonnaise dressing, beets, and nuts. Divide into wet individual molds and set away to firm. Turn out on the shredded lettuce or cabbage and serve with dressing.

Imperial Salad

Melted aspic jelly	½ pint (1 cup) cooked
Watercress	string-beans
12 heads cooked asparagus	Mayonnaise dressing
2 cooked potatoes	1 hard-cooked egg
½ pint (1 cup) cooked	
green peas	

Line a plain, wet ring mold with aspic jelly, decorate with leaves of watercress, fill up with aspic jelly, put in a cool place until set, then turn out and decorate the outside base with the white of egg cut in small pieces.

Dice the potatoes and mix with them the heads of asparagus, peas, beans, and mayonnaise. Turn into the center of the aspic mold, and decorate with the yolk of egg rubbed through a sieve.

Canned asparagus may be used.

Italian Salad

2 cold boiled potatoes	Anchovies
1 cooked beet	Pickles or olives
Mixed cooked vegetables	Tartare sauce
Ham, fowl, or game	

Cut the potatoes and beet in slices one-half inch thick, cut them into neat round shapes with a cutter, and put them into a salad bowl with equal quantities of green peas, sprigs of cauliflower, asparagus tips, string-beans, diced celery, Brussels sprouts, beans or lentils, according to what is in season; add to these a little shredded cooked ham, fowl, or game, anchovies, pickles, or olives, and mix with tartare sauce.

If liked, the salad bowl may be rubbed with a cut clove of garlic.

Jellied Fruit and Celery Salad

Sour lemon jelly	Apples
Few drops red color	Oranges
Crisp lettuce leaves	Fresh or canned pineapple
Stiff mayonnaise dressing	Celery
Blanched English walnut meats	Whipped cream

Slice or shred the fruits and celery into small wet molds. Fill up with the lemon jelly colored red with red coloring and set away to firm. Turn out at serving time on the lettuce leaves, decorate with the walnut meats, and serve with stiff mayonnaise to which whipped cream has been added.

Jellied Ham Salad

½ pint (1 cup) chopped cooked ham	½ pint (1 cup) whipped cream
½ teaspoonful paprika	1½ gills (¾ cup) stock
½ teaspoonful onion-juice	2 tablespoonfuls water
1 teaspoonful made mustard	Crisp lettuce leaves
1 tablespoonful gelatine	Mayonnaise dressing

Soak the gelatine in the water, then dissolve it in the stock over the fire; strain over the ham, add the seasonings, and stir over chopped ice until it begins to thicken; then stir in the whipped cream. Pour into a wet ring mold. Turn out on to crisp lettuce leaves, fill the center with heart lettuce leaves, and cover these with mayonnaise dressing.

Kumquat Salad

12 kumquats	1 banana
1 canned pear	Lettuce leaves
1 apple	French dressing
1 shredded green pepper	1 grapefruit

Cut up the kumquats, free them from skin and seeds, add the pear cut in dice, the apple cored, peeled, and cut in cubes, the pulp of the grapefruit, the pepper, and the banana peeled and cut into small pieces. Mix with French dressing and serve on the lettuce leaves.

Another Method.—Line a salad bowl with endive or lettuce hearts and arrange in it a layer of thinly sliced apple; sprinkle over a little lemon-juice, than a layer of thinly sliced kumquats, then a layer of skinned and seeded grapes, and sprinkle over with chopped pecan nut meats. Serve with boiled dressing to which one cupful of whipped cream has been added.

Lobster Salad No. 1

1 cooked lobster	Shredded lettuce leaves
2 ozs. (4 tablespoonfuls) butter	Paprika
	Lobster coral
Fresh mushrooms	Mayonnaise dressing
1 lemon	Capers

Divide the meat of the lobster into small pieces. Melt the butter, add the lobster, and fry it for a few minutes with about one-half its quantity of mushrooms cut in quarters. Drain, cool, and arrange on the lettuce in a salad dish, season with lemon-juice and paprika, and cover with a mayonnaise dressing. Decorate with capers and lobster coral.

Another Method.—Cut the meat of a cooked lobster into thin strips, then into dice. Season with two tablespoonfuls of vinegar, three tablespoonfuls of oil, and salt and pepper to taste. Add one tablespoonful of chopped olives and a chopped dill pickle. Mix with mayonnaise and serve on lettuce leaves, with a garnish of stiff mayonnaise and claws from the lobster.

Lobster Salad No. 2

1 cooked lobster	Anchovy fillets
Shredded lettuce	A medium-sized gherkin or
Mayonnaise dressing	sweet pickle

Remove the flesh of the lobster from the shell and cut or break it into neat pieces. Brush over the shell while it is hot with salad oil, and wipe or brush it off again. Wash, dry, and shred the lettuce and put some of it into a salad dish; then some slices of the lobster, and coat them with mayonnaise dressing. Add more lettuce and lobster and dressing until all are used. Put the head end of the shell cut one-fourth of an inch from the eyes at one end of the salad and the tail at the other end. Make a latticework at one side with anchovy fillets, and place the gherkin cut like a fan at the other. Keep on ice until required.

Mint Salad

Shredded lettuce	Chopped cooked lamb or
Chopped mint	chicken
	French dressing

Wash, dry, and shred some young lettuce and sprinkle it liberally with chopped mint. Cover with a layer of chopped cooked lamb or chicken and cover with French dressing. Garnish with sprigs of mint and serve.

Another Method.—Mix two cupfuls of diced cold lamb with one cupful of cold sliced potatoes, season with salt and red pepper, and mix with mayonnaise dressing. Garnish with slices of hard-cooked eggs and mint jelly cut in squares.

Lettuce Salad and Roquefort Dressing

Lettuce hearts	3 tablespoonfuls vinegar
1 clove garlic	Olive oil
¼ teaspoonful dry mustard	3 tablespoonfuls Roquefort cheese
1 saltspoonful salt	2 hard-cooked eggs
1 saltspoonful paprika	

Place the lettuce hearts in a salad bowl which has been rubbed over with the cut clove of garlic. Mix together the mustard, salt, paprika, vinegar, and beat in olive oil until thick; then gradually add the cheese and the hard-cooked yolks of eggs rubbed through a sieve.

Pour over the lettuce and serve garnished with the whites of eggs cut in rings.

Merry Maze Salad

Romaine lettuce	Cucumber peel
Grapefruit	Cream cheese
Oranges	Chopped green peppers
Pimientoes	French dressing

Place three or four long stalks of crisp Romaine lettuce on individual salad plates, lay across sections of grapefruit and oranges; then place two strips of pimientoes lengthwise on the oranges and grapefruit, and garnish with tiny spirals of green cucumber peel. Cover with French dressing, and on each plate place a ball of the cream cheese into which pieces of the green peppers have been creamed.

French or Belgian endive may be used in place of the Romaine.

Nut and Prune Salad

1 lb. large prunes	Crisp lettuce leaves
Chopped English walnut meats	Mayonnaise dressing

Wash, soak, and cook the prunes until tender. Drain, and when cold, pit and fill the cavities with chopped nut meats. Serve four of these stuffed prunes in nests of lettuce and cover with mayonnaise dressing made with lemon-juice.

Another Method.—Pit some cold cooked prunes and cut each in four pieces lengthwise. Mix with half the quantity of broken nut meats and serve on lettuce leaves covered with whipped cream seasoned to taste with salt and paprika.

Nut Salad

½ pint (1 cup) chopped
mixed nut meats
½ pint (1 cup) shredded
celery
Lettuce leaves

½ pint (1 cup) seeded
grapes
1 orange
Boiled dressing
Whole nut meats

Mix the nut meats, celery, and grapes with the strained orange-juice. Serve on lettuce leaves, decorate with the whole nut meats and boiled dressing.

Or, mix one cupful each of chopped hickorynuts and almonds, two cupfuls of chopped celery, and one cupful of whipped cream with boiled salad dressing. Chill and serve.

Okra Salad

2 dozen cooked okra pods
4 skinned and sliced tomatoes
Mayonnaise dressing

2 green peppers cut in
shreds
Boiled rice
Crisp lettuce leaves

Cut the okra pods into neat pieces, add the tomatoes and peppers. Arrange boiled rice in a border on a salad dish, put the okra in the center, and garnish with lettuce leaves mixed with mayonnaise dressing.

Orange and Tomato Salad

3 peeled and sliced tomatoes	½ teaspoonful sugar
3 peeled and sliced oranges	½ teaspoonful chopped tarragon
½ lemon, peeled and sliced	½ teaspoonful chopped chives
Salt and paprika to taste	4 tablespoonfuls olive oil
	4 tablespoonfuls brandy

Mix the fruits, season with salt and paprika, add the sugar, tarragon, and chives. Mix the oil and the brandy together, add them to the salad, and mix well.

Grapefruit, if liked, may be substituted for the oranges.

Another Method.—Peel some oranges and tomatoes and slice them; then arrange alternately in a salad bowl. Mix equal quantities of orange-juice and tarragon vinegar with a little salad oil, and pour over the fruit. Decorate with chopped parsley and serve very cold.

Oyster and Egg Salad

2 dozen oysters	1 tablespoonful tomato catchup
6 hard-cooked eggs	1 teaspoonful chili powder
4 tablespoonfuls vinegar	½ teaspoonful salt
1 tablespoonful melted butter	Shredded celery and celery tops
½ lemon	

Dry the oysters and place them on the ice. Rub the yolks of eggs through a sieve, add the butter, vinegar, catchup, salt, chili powder, and strained lemon-juice. Toss the oysters in the sauce and serve them on shredded celery garnished with celery tops.

The whites of eggs may be used in another salad or in sandwiches.

Another Method.—Parboil two cupfuls of oysters. Drain, cut into quarters, drain again, and cover with French dressing. Serve on watercress in individual dishes with sauce tartare.

Or, if preferred, have a mayonnaise dressing and into it stir a little grated horseradish and two drops of Tabasco sauce.

Park Lane Salad

Apples	Chopped nut meats
Celery	Toasted crackers
Mayonnaise dressing	Cream cheese
Pimientoes	

Cut some apples and celery in small cubes, mix equal quantities with nicely seasoned mayonnaise dressing. Serve in individual salad plates, decorated with strips of pimientoes and chopped nuts. Cream cheese and toasted crackers are a suitable accompaniment for this salad.

Olive and Celery Salad

1 crisp head lettuce	1 teaspoonful mustard
1 bunch watercress	½ teaspoonful salt
1 green onion	2 teaspoonfuls sugar
1 pint (2 cups) chopped olives	2 tablespoonfuls vinegar
½ pint (1 cup) chopped celery	2 ozs. (4 tablespoonfuls) butter
2 skinned tomatoes	1 raw egg
3 hard-cooked eggs	4 tablespoonfuls cream

Cut the onion, lettuce, and watercress in fine pieces, add the olives, celery, the tomatoes cut in pieces, and one of the hard-cooked yolks of eggs rubbed through a sieve. Mix and put away to chill. Put the mustard, salt, and sugar into a double boiler, add the vinegar, butter, and egg well beaten, and cook and stir until thick. Cool, add the cream, and pour over the salad. Serve garnished with the hard-cooked eggs.

Pea and Pickle Salad

½ pint (1 cup) cooked peas	6 sweet pickles
2 tablespoonfuls grated cheese	1 small onion
	Mayonnaise dressing
	Crisp lettuce leaves

Chop the onion and the pickles, add the peas and cheese, moisten with the mayonnaise dressing, and serve on the lettuce leaves.

Another Method.—Mix a can of drained peas with one cupful of chopped peanuts and six chopped sweet pickles; moisten with mayonnaise dressing and serve on tender lettuce leaves.

Oyster Salad

1 can oysters	¾ teaspoonful black
1 pint (2 cups) cracker-	pepper
crumbs	½ pint (1 cup) chopped
1 gill (½ cup) vinegar	celery
1 tablespoonful salt	5 hard-cooked eggs,
2 tablespoons sugar	chopped

Chop the oysters fine, and add the cracker-crumbs, salt, sugar, pepper, and vinegar. Mix well, and add the eggs, celery, and enough of the oyster liquor to make soft. Serve very cold.

Another Method.—Pour oysters and juice from one can into a salad dish, cut up the oysters, add enough rolled crackers to take up all the liquid, then add one bunch of celery, chopped, six chopped sweet pickles, three chopped hard-cooked eggs, and one-half cupful of chopped nut meats. Pour over thick mayonnaise dressing, and decorate with heart lettuce leaves.

Pea and Walnut Salad

1 pint (2 cups) blanched	Salt to taste
English walnut meats	Crisp lettuce leaves
1 pint (2 cups) cooked or	Boiled dressing
canned peas	Mint leaves
1 large green pepper	

Chop the pepper fine and chop the nut meats, then mix them with the peas and add salt to taste. Arrange on crisp lettuce leaves on a salad dish, cover with the dressing, and garnish with the mint leaves.

Equal quantities of blanched and broken English walnut meats and stoned and quartered olives mixed with French dressing make a dainty salad when served in lettuce nests.

Peanut and Celery Salad

½ pint (1 cup) peanuts	12 pitted or stuffed olives
Olive oil	Mayonnaise dressing
1 pint (2 cups) fine cut celery	Lettuce leaves

Soak the peanuts from which the brown skins have been removed in sufficient olive oil to moisten, for two hours. Slice the olives, add the celery and peanuts, mix with mayonnaise dressing, and serve on crisp lettuce leaves.

It is much easier to serve a salad if the lettuce leaves are put together in such a way as to form little cups or nests. Equal quantities of diced crisp celery and diced canned pineapple mixed with mayonnaise dressing make a delicious salad.

Another Method.—Pare, core, and chop slightly acid apples and mix with them one-half as much chopped white celery. Mix five tablespoonfuls of lemon-juice with one tablespoonful of peanut butter, and salt and red pepper to taste, and mix with the apples and celery. Chill and serve on lettuce leaves garnished with halves of roasted peanuts.

Peach Salad

1 can peaches	Salt, black pepper, and red pepper to taste
3 ripe bananas	
1 egg	Grated cheese
1 tablespoonful vinegar	1 gill (½ cup) whipped cream
Sugar to taste	

Drain the peaches and lay them on a salad dish. Beat up the egg in a small pan, add the vinegar, and cook until thick, stirring constantly. Add the seasonings, then cool and add the cream. Dice the bananas, mix them with the dressing, and divide into the hollows of the peaches. Cover with grated cheese and serve.

Another Method.—Place two eggs into the upper pan of a double boiler, add four tablespoonfuls of vinegar, one-fourth teaspoonful of mustard, one-fourth teaspoonful of salt, and one teaspoonful of sugar. Cook and stir until thick and then allow to cool. Add one cupful of whipped cream and one can of sliced pineapple cut into dice. Cover individual salad plates with shredded lettuce; on this lay half of one peach, and cover with the pineapple dressing. Sprinkle over with chopped nuts or chopped glacé cherries. Or fill canned peaches with cottage cheese, place on lettuce leaves, and cover with boiled salad dressing.

Pimiento Salad

Pimientoes	Mayonnaise dressing
Grapefruit	English walnut meats
Oranges	Lettuce

Cover individual salad plates with shredded lettuce leaves. Empty out the pimientoes and wipe them off gently with a clean cloth. Stuff them with diced grapefruit and oranges mixed with mayonnaise dressing. Place them on the lettuce leaves and decorate with the walnut meats.

Pineapple and Grapefruit Salad

Sliced pineapple	English walnut meats
Small grapefruit	French dressing
Strawberries	

Choose well-shaped grapefruit and cut in halves crosswise. Remove the hard piece of core and the seeds; with a teaspoon scoop out all the pulp, including the juice. Drop the shells into ice water. Take the sliced pineapple, invert a glass or cup over each portion, and, with a very sharp pointed knife cut all the way around. Put the slices to marinate in French dressing made with part lemon, grapefruit juice and olive oil. Set in a cold place for one hour. Mix the small pieces of pineapple and grapefruit together, when ready to use, with a few strawberries cut in halves. Mix with the dressing and divide into the grapefruit shells, and lay on top of the slice of pineapple, which has been cut in small pieces, but laid together again to make the slice complete. Sprinkle the top with nut meats cut fine, and in the center place the strawberries. Serve on plates covered with doilies.

Fruit salad or cream mayonnaise dressing may be used instead of French dressing.

Or place slices of pineapple on crisp lettuce leaves on individual salad plates, top with sections of grapefruit and oranges, cover with the following dressing and sprinkle over with blanched and chopped pistachio nuts. Dressing—Beat six tablespoonfuls of olive oil with two tablespoonfuls of lemon-juice, one tablespoonful of sherry wine and one-fourth teaspoonful each of salt and paprika.

Pear Salad

Canned pears	Chopped preserved ginger
Chopped raisins	Whipped and sweetened
Chopped figs	cream
Chopped dates	Candied cherries
Chopped nuts	Ferns or grape leaves

Drain the pears and lay them on ferns or grape leaves on individual salad plates. Mix equal quantities of the raisins, figs, dates, nuts, and ginger, and heap into the pears. Top each one with whipped cream and a candied cherry.

Another Method.—Fill large fresh or canned pears with a mixture of chopped celery and English walnut meats mixed with red mayonnaise dressing. Serve with cream cheese balls seasoned with paprika.

Or take quarters of canned pears and sprinkle over with orange-juice. Place balls of cream cheese seasoned with salt and paprika in the center of the pears. Place on lettuce or endive, and pour over the following dressing: Beat one-fourth cupful of olive oil with two teaspoonfuls of vinegar, one-half teaspoonful each of salt and mustard, one-half teaspoonful of paprika, a dust of red pepper, and one-half cupful of chili sauce, and when well blended, add one-half cupful of mayonnaise dressing very slowly. Decorate the salad with shreds of red peppers or stars of pimientoes.

Queen Salad

½ can pimientoes	Cracker crumbs
Celery	2 yolks hard-cooked eggs
½ pint (1 cup) tiny cheese	French dressing
balls	Crisp lettuce leaves

Drain the peppers and dry them in a towel. Slice them in rings and add an equal quantity of celery cut fine. Make the cheese balls and roll them in the cracker-crumbs. Blend the oil from the peppers with the yolks of the eggs. Rub the salad bowl with a cut clove of garlic, put in the peppers, celery, and cheese balls, and pour over the oil and egg mixture. Toss together with sufficient French dressing and a few crisp lettuce leaves.

Potato Salad No. 1

Boiled potatoes	1 pickled herring
1 small onion	1 tablespoonful chopped
1 pickled beet	boiled ham
1 sliced cucumber	1 tablespoonful vinegar
4 sardines	1 pickled walnut

Peel small boiled potatoes while warm, slice very thin, and, for every two cupfuls of potatoes, add a chopped onion, diced pickled beet, cucumber, herring, sardines broken in small pieces, and the ham. Mix together with the vinegar. Serve garnished with the pickled walnut cut in small pieces.

Another Method.—To two cupfuls of left-over mashed potatoes, add two and one-half tablespoonfuls of melted butter, two tablespoonfuls of chopped parsley, salt to taste, two teaspoonfuls of onion-juice, and two tablespoonfuls of vinegar. Mix and chill. Shape into balls, place on lettuce leaves, and serve with boiled salad dressing.

Potato Salad No. 2

Boiled potatoes	French dressing
Onions	1 clove
Chopped parsley or chives	

Boil as many peeled potatoes as needed with an onion stuck with a clove. When tender, remove from the water and let cool, throwing the onion away. When cold, slice as thin as possible; also slice one small onion for every two potatoes. Mix carefully, sprinkle with a little chopped parsley or chives, chill, and when ready to serve pour over French dressing.

To make *hot potato salad:* Prepare the potatoes as above directed, then chop the onions and mix them with the potatoes. Cut four slices of bacon in dice and fry brown. Remove the meat and stir into the hot fat four tablespoonfuls of vinegar. Mix the bacon with the potato and onion, and pour over all the hot sauce. Serve hot.

Potato Salad No. 3

1 quart cold boiled potatoes	2 tablespoonfuls butter
2 tablespoonfuls capers	1 teaspoonful made mustard
2 tablespoonfuls chopped parsley	4 tablespoonfuls vinegar
1 slice onion	1 saltspoonful salt
Boiled beets	Pepper and paprika to taste
	Lettuce leaves

Rub the salad bowl with the onion, and into it put the potatoes that have been diced. Stir the capers and the parsley through the potatoes. Melt the butter, add the seasonings and vinegar, and heat to boiling-point. Pour over the potatoes while the sauce is hot, and set away to get cold. Arrange on lettuce leaves, sprinkling the beets, finely chopped, over the top.

Radish Salad

3 bunches radishes	Mayonnaise dressing
Crisp lettuce leaves	

Cut the stems from the radishes, wash carefully, and chop them into dice with the red skins left on. Mix with mayonnaise dressing and serve on the lettuce leaves.

Another Method.—Mix equal quantities of cleaned and sliced radishes and peeled and diced apples, marinate in French dressing, drain, and mix with boiled dressing. Serve on watercress or lettuce leaves. Sliced radishes blend nicely with chopped chives and French dressing.

Red Kidney Bean Salad

1 can red kidney beans	2½ teaspoonfuls made
2 stalks sliced celery	mustard
5 sliced sweet pickles	1½ gills (¾ cup) cider
1 egg	vinegar
2 teaspoonfuls sugar	2 teaspoonfuls Worcestershire sauce

Drain the beans and mix them with the celery and the pickles. Beat up the egg, add the sugar, mustard, salt, vinegar, and Worcestershire sauce. Mix the salad with this dressing and set in a cool place for three hours before serving.

Romaine Salad

Crisp Romaine leaves	¼ teaspoonful mustard
6 tablespoonfuls salad oil	¼ teaspoonful salt
3 tablespoonfuls claret vinegar	¼ teaspoonful sugar
	¼ teaspoonful black pepper

Wash and dry the Romaine leaves and arrange them in a chilled salad bowl. Put the oil, vinegar, and seasonings into a bowl and mix them with a piece of ice. Pour this dressing over the Romaine a few minutes before it is to be served.

Salad of Fruits Glace

2 egg whites	Small bunches fruits
2 wineglassfuls water	Whipped cream
2 dessertspoonfuls confectioners' sugar	Pink or green color
Hot sifted granulated sugar	Fruit syrup
	Liqueur

Beat up the whites of eggs to a stiff froth, add the water and stir in the confectioners' sugar, and strain through a fine sieve into a basin. Have ready the fruits, such as bunches of red and white currants, small bunches of grapes, cherries, strawberries, slices of oranges, etc.; dip them into the icing, give them a gentle shake, and roll them carefully and thoroughly in plenty of hot sifted white sugar; place them upon a wire sieve in a warm oven to dry, when they will present a very dainty appearance. Arrange them in pyramid form in the center of a glass dish, surrounding them with a border of whipped and sweetened cream, colored pink or green, according to taste. Hand round with this salad a fruit syrup flavored with any liqueur preferred.

Salmon and Oyster Salad

1 lb. cooked or canned salmon	Salad oil
12 oysters	Vinegar
¼ pint (½ cup) picked shrimps	1 tablespoonful chopped tarragon
6 filleted anchovies	½ tablespoonful chopped chervil
2 hard-cooked eggs	Tomato salad dressing
1 cucumber	Pepper and salt
2 heads of lettuce	

First make the tomato salad dressing. Beat two raw yolks of eggs, add gradually one-half cupful of salad oil, salt and pepper to taste, one teaspoonful of French mustard, one dessertspoonful of vinegar, the pulp from two large ripe tomatoes, and the strained juice of one lemon. Mix well.

Cut the heads of lettuce into six pieces, and lay them on a plate; sprinkle them over with the tarragon and chervil and season to taste with oil, vinegar, salt, and pepper. Arrange this salad as a border on the serving dish.

Flake the salmon, add the oysters, shrimps, and the anchovies cut in small pieces. Place this mixture in the center of the pieces of lettuce, and pour over the dressing. Garnish around the edge of the salad with slices of the hard-cooked eggs and little bunches of diced-shaped pieces of the cucumber that have been seasoned with a little salt.

Sardine Salad

1 can sardines	4 cucumbers
2 apples	2 hard-cooked eggs
¼ pint (½ cup) celery	Salt, pepper, and paprika
2 ozs. (½ cup) pecan nut	tc taste
meats	Mayonnaise dressing
4 potatoes	Crisp lettuce leaves

Pare and core the apples and chop them with the celery, nut meats, eggs, and cucumbers. Boil the potatoes until done and mash fine with the sardines, then add seasonings and mix with mayonnaise dressing. Combine mixtures. Serve cold on lettuce leaves.

Saratoga Salad

1 pint (2 cups) chopped cooked ham	1 gill (½ cup) cream
	Boiled dressing
1½ pints (3 cups) cottage cheese	Lettuce leaves
	Cubes tomato jelly
4 ozs. (1 cup) nut meats	

Put the cheese and ham each through a meat-chopper; moisten the cheese with the cream, add the ham and a little salt if necessary. Add enough boiled salad dressing to form into balls the size of a walnut. Roll in the finely chopped nut meats, and serve three balls on a lettuce leaf garnished with cubes of tomato jelly.

Scallop Salad

1 pint (2 cups) scallops	Chopped olives
½ pint (1 cup) diced celery	Chopped chives
	Chopped gherkins
French or mayonnaise dressing	Chopped hard-cooked egg
	Watercress

Soak the scallops in salted water for one hour. Drain and boil for five minutes in slightly acidulated boiling water, then plunge in ice water. When cold, cut in thin slices, add the celery, and mix with the dressing.

Serve on watercress, garnishing with the olives, chives, gherkins, and egg mixed together.

The scallops may be mixed with shredded cabbage, shredded lettuce, chopped green peppers, or peeled and sliced cucumbers.

Shrimp, Celery and Nut Salad

½ pint (1 cup) cooked or canned shrimps
½ pint (1 cup) broken pecan nut meats
½ pint (1 cup) chopped celery
4 sliced hard-cooked eggs
½ teaspoonful salt
Paprika to taste
2 lemons
3 tablespoonfuls olive oil
Pickled beets
Crisp lettuce leaves

Mix the shrimps with the nuts, celery, and salt. Rub the yolks of eggs through a sieve, add salt and paprika to taste, the oil, and the strained juice of the lemons. Beat for five minutes and pour over the salad on lettuce leaves. Garnish with the rings of hard-cooked eggs and slices of beets.

Spanish Onion and Sardine Salad

3 medium-sized Spanish onions
Butter
Watercress
6 sardines
Mayonnaise dressing
Curry powder
Hard-cooked eggs
Parsley and tarragon
Salt and paprika to taste

Peel the onions, scoop a spoonful out of the center of each, and put in the hollow a generous teaspoonful of butter. Season with salt and paprika to taste, place in a buttered baking-pan, and bake in a moderate oven until they are brown. When cold, cut into quarters and place in a bed of watercress.

Skin and bone the sardines, cut them into halves, and lay them on the pieces of onion. Pour over some mayonnaise dressing to one cupful of which one teaspoonful of curry powder has been added. Garnish with the eggs cut in slices, and sprinkle over a mixture of chopped parsley and tarragon.

Salmon Salad

1 can salmon	½ pint (1 cup) diced
1 diced apple	celery
½ pint (1 cup) broken	Crisp lettuce leaves
English walnut meats	Mayonnaise dressing
2 chopped gherkins	½ pint (1 cup) whipped
Lemon-juice	cream

Free the salmon from oil, skin, and bones; pick the fish apart and add the apple, sprinkled with lemon-juice, walnut meats, chopped gherkins, and the celery. Arrange in a salad dish, garnish with lettuce leaves, and serve with mayonnaise to which has been added the cream.

Another Method.—Wash and dry two heads of lettuce. Dip the outer leaves in oil and vinegar and lay them in the salad bowl. On this lay a ring of pieces of cold boiled salmon, cover it with mayonnaise dressing; place the heart of the lettuce in the center, pour a little mayonnaise over it, and garnish with rings of hard-cooked eggs and slices of cooked beets.

Spinach Salad

Cold boiled spinach	Lettuce leaves
Salt and pepper to taste	Hard-cooked eggs
Grated nutmeg to taste	Salad dressing

Chop the spinach, season with salt, pepper, and nutmeg and mold in small buttered cups. Turn out at serving time on lettuce leaves and garnish with hard-cooked eggs sliced, or with the yolks put through a ricer. Strips of canned red peppers may be used as a garnish if preferred. Serve with mayonnaise or French dressing.

Another Method.—Cook one-half peck of spinach; chop when cold, and add salt, pepper, and grated nutmeg to taste, five tablespoonfuls of olive oil, and then beat in three table-spoonfuls of vinegar. Mold the spinach in a ring on a salad dish, fill the center with slices of hard-cooked eggs, and surround with thin slices of cold boiled ham.

Strawberry Salad

1 pint (2 cups) ripe straw-berries	1 teaspoonful white pepper
1 gill (½ cup) chopped nut meats	1 teaspoonful sugar
½ pint (1 cup) celery cubes	2 tablespoonfuls lemon- or other fruit-juice
½ teaspoonful salt	4 tablespoonfuls olive oil
1 saltspoonful paprika	Crisp lettuce

Arrange three of the inner leaves of head lettuce on each salad plate, sprinkle in a layer of nut meats, place a few strawberries in the center, add a layer of celery cubes, and cover with the following dressing. Mix the salt, peppers, and sugar with the lemon-juice, add gradually the oil. Beat well together and pour over the fruit. A little whipped cream may be added to the dressing before serving.

Or mash one pound of small strawberries with a silver fork, and sprinkle a little sugar over them; let them stand in a cool place for two hours, then add two cupfuls of sherry wine and rub all through a sieve. Pile large ripe strawberries pyramid fashion on a pretty glass dish, and sprinkle a little powdered cinnamon over them; then pour over the mashed mixture.

Or mix one quart of strawberries cut in halves with one-half pound of marshmallows cut in quarters and one-half cupful of blanched and chopped pistachio nuts, and serve on lettuce leaves with whipped cream dressing.

String-Bean Salad

2 quarts string-beans	4 tablespoonfuls olive oil
1 onion	½ teaspoon mustard
Shredded lettuce leaves	Paprika to taste
2 tablespoonfuls claret vinegar	1 small chopped green pepper

Put the beans and onion into plenty of boiling salted water and cook until tender. Discard the onion, drain the beans, and let them get quite cold. Mix the oil with the vinegar, add the mustard, paprika, and the pepper. Place the beans on the lettuce, pour the dressing over, and let stand on ice for one hour before serving.

Stuffed Tomato Salad

Medium-sized tomatoes   Caviar
Chopped cucumbers   Oil and vinegar
Chopped chives   Lettuce or watercress

Peel the tomatoes and take from the stem-end of each a round piece for a lid for later use. Scoop out the tomatoes, and to the pulp add some chopped cucumber, chopped chives, and caviar. Season to taste with oil, vinegar, salt, and black pepper. Chill, divide into the tomato shells, and serve in individual dishes on watercress or shredded lettuce.

Another Method.—Season skinned tomato shells with vinegar, salt, and paprika and drain them well. Cut two cupfuls of asparagus tips into small pieces, boil them in boiling salted water until tender, and drain. Add grated nutmeg, paprika, and red pepper to taste, and mix with tartare sauce. Divide into the prepared tomatoes and cover the surface with a little mayonnaise dressing. Garnish with sliced stuffed olives and serve.

Or fill the tomato shells with cooked or canned corn, mixed with chopped green or red peppers and seasoned with French dressing. Top with mayonnaise dressing and place in lettuce leaves. Chill before serving.

Sweetbread Salad

1 pair cooked sweetbreads   4 tablespoonfuls chopped
1 cup chopped celery   nut meats
4 hard-cooked eggs   Mayonnaise dressing

Chop the eggs and shred the sweetbreads, mix them together with the celery, nuts, and mayonnaise dressing.

Another Method.—Mix one cupful of diced cooked sweetbreads with one cupful of cooked and drained peas and one cupful of shredded celery. Serve on lettuce leaves with mayonnaise dressing.

Tomato Jelly Salad

1 pint tomato juice
¾ oz. (2¼ tablespoonfuls)
   powdered gelatine
¼ pint (½ cup) water
¼ teaspoonful celery seeds
1 tablespoonful onion-
   juice
2 bay-leaves
3 cloves
1 teaspoonful salt
¼ teaspoonful paprika
A few drops red color

1 tablespoonful chopped
   parsley
1 tablespoonful vinegar
1 tablespoonful lemon-
   juice
½ pint (½ cup) cooked
   chopped meat
1 blade mace
Mayonnaise dressing
½ pint (1 cup) whipped
   cream
Lettuce leaves

Put into a saucepan the tomato juice, gelatine, water, celery seeds, onion-juice, bay-leaves, cloves, mace, salt, and paprika, and bring to boiling-point; then strain. Add the parsley, red color, vinegar, lemon-juice, meat, and cream. Pour into a wet ring mold, and set away to firm. Turn out on a salad dish, fill the center with lettuce leaves, and serve with the mayonnaise dressing.

Tongue Salad

1 small boiled beef tongue
Salt and pepper to taste
½ pint (1 cup) chopped
   celery or cabbage
3 chopped hard-cooked
   eggs
3 chopped cucumber
   pickles

2 tablespoonfuls sugar
1 tablespoonful flour
¼ teaspoonful mustard
1 beaten egg
1½ gills (¾ cup) vinegar
½ gill (¼ cup) water
1 gill (½ cup) sweet
   cream

Put the tongue through a food-chopper, add the celery, eggs, and pickles; add a little salt and pepper and set in a cool place. Mix the sugar and flour together in a small saucepan, add one teaspoonful of salt, one-eighth teaspoonful pepper, the mustard, egg, vinegar, and water. Cook and stir until it thickens. Cool, add the cream, and mix with the salad.

Another Method.—Mix two cupfuls of diced cooked tongue with one cupful of diced celery, add one cupful of chopped nut meats and a small can of chopped pimientoes. Mix with mayonnaise dressing and serve on crisp lettuce leaves.

Tripe Salad

Pickled tripe   Chopped olives
Mayonnaise dressing   Chopped capers
Chopped parsley   Chopped gherkins

Cut the required amount of pickled tripe into fine strips. Make a good mayonnaise dressing, and add to it chopped parsley, olives, capers, and gherkins to taste. Mix the tripe with the dressing and serve on lettuce leaves.

Another Method.—Mix diced cooked tripe with an equal quantity of finely cut celery, add one tablespoonful of capers, and mix with mayonnaise or French dressing. Serve on endive garnished with stoned olives or slices of hard-cooked eggs.

Anchovy and Walnut Salad

1 head celery   Mayonnaise dressing
2 heads of endive   6 olives
14 English walnuts   6 anchovies

Chop the celery, cut the hearts of the endives into small pieces, add the walnuts peeled and broken into small pieces, mix with a good mayonnaise dressing, and serve garnished with the olives and the anchovies cut into fillets.

Tuna Fish Salad

1 can tuna   2 tablespoonfuls lemon-
Shredded lettuce   juice
Salt and red pepper   Mayonnaise dressing
1 tablespoonful vinegar   1 tablespoonful capers
1 hard-cooked egg   2 or 3 stuffed olives

Line a salad dish with shredded lettuce. Break the fish into pieces and place it on the top of the lettuce. Mix the salt, red pepper, lemon-juice, and vinegar together and pour over the fish. Chill, and when ready to serve, decorate with the capers, slices of hard-cooked egg, and the stuffed olives. Serve with mayonnaise dressing.

Another Method.—Flake one can of the tuna with a silver fork, add one and one-half cupful of diced celery and one-half cupful of broken English walnut meats, mix with mayonnaise— or boiled dressing. Serve on crisp lettuce leaves.

Turnip Salad

1 quart (4 cups) scraped turnips	1 egg white
	1 gill (½ cup) vinegar
1 oz. (2 tablespoonfuls) sugar	1 tablespoonful water
	1 tablespoonful cornstarch
2 tablespoonfuls cream	1 tablespoonful butter

Select medium-sized good turnips and peel and scrape them. Put the fluffy scraped turnip into a dish, and add the sugar, cream, and stiffly beaten white of egg. Mix the cornstarch with the water in a saucepan, add the vinegar and the butter, and stir constantly over the fire until it thickens; pour hot over the turnips and mix well. Leave in a cool place for two hours before serving.

Macaroni Salad

½ pound (58 sticks) macaroni	1 teaspoonful sugar
	½ teaspoonful salt
2½ tablespoonfuls fresh grated horseradish	1 pint whipped cream
	Crisp lettuce leaves

Break the macaroni into small pieces, boil in plenty of boiling salted water until tender, then drain and cool. Mix the horseradish with the sugar, salt, and whipped cream; fold in the macaroni and serve heaped on the lettuce leaves.

Another Method.—Boil one package of macaroni, then rinse it with cold water and drain. Cut it into short lengths, place one-half of it in a jar of vinegar in which boiled beets have been pickled, and let it remain until colored a pretty pink.

Line a salad dish with crisp lettuce leaves and arrange the pink and white macaroni in alternate rings. Garnish with sprigs of parsley and tiny leaves of lettuce. Serve with boiled salad dressing.

Spaghetti may be used in the same way.

Vegetable Salad in Shells

Cold cooked vegetables	Boned anchovies
Chopped parsley	Picked shrimps
Chopped shallot	Thick mayonnaise dressing
Vinegar and salad oil	Shredded celery
Skinned and sliced toma-	Red radishes
toes	Lettuce or endive

Take some cold cooked vegetables, such as potatoes, carrots, turnips, peas, beans, cauliflower, and Brussels sprouts; cut these all separately into little square pieces and put them into a basin, seasoning with a little salt, sugar, pepper, parsley, shallot, vinegar, and oil.

Have some ramequins or scallop shells, and in each arrange a tablespoonful of the prepared vegetables. Season the tomatoes with oil, vinegar, salt, and pepper, and arrange a slice on the top of each of the servings; put here and there around the vegetables one or two washed and boned anchovies, and a few of the shrimps, and form the whole into a dome shape.

Spread the mayonnaise dressing over the servings, and decorate with the celery and the radishes that have been cut into roses. Serve the ramequins on a flat dish with attractive garnishing in the center, allowing for one to each person.

Cordial Salad

Bananas	Grapes
Stoned cherries	Apples
Diced pineapple	Plums
Melon	Pears
Peaches	Ginger cordial
Apricots	Sugar

Prepare the fruits and slice and dice them. Cover one pound of sugar with one pint of water and cook until the syrup is thick and ropy. Cool and flavor to taste with ginger cordial. Any other preferred cordial or liqueur may be used.

Mix the fruits in a salad bowl decorated with cherries, and serve with the flavored syrup.

Waldorf Salad

Apples	Curled celery
Celery	Pimientoes
Mayonnaise dressing	Lettuce leaves

Mix equal quantities of finely cut apples and celery, and moisten with mayonnaise dressing. Place in lettuce and garnish with curled celery and pimientoes cut in strips or fancy shapes, or with hazelnuts and maraschino cherries cut in halves. An attractive way of serving this salad is to remove the tips from red or green polished apples, scoop out the pulp, leaving just enough adhering to the skin to keep the apples in shape. Refill the shells thus made with the salad, replace the tops and serve on crisp lettuce leaves.

Red apple shells are delicious filled with the following mixtures: Salted almonds mixed with peeled white grapes, cubes of pineapple, and mayonnaise dressing. Garnish the top with candied rose leaves and serve the apple cases on grape leaves.

Cold green peas, mixed with cut celery, and diced cold chicken and boiled dressing. Top with very thin slices of lemon and chopped parsley and garnish with radish roses.

Watermelon Salad

1 watermelon	1 gill (½ cup) olive oil
Spanish onions	3 tablespoonfuls vinegar
Salt, pepper, and paprika to taste	½ gill (¼ cup) lemon-juice

Peel and slice the melon into a deep dish, add some thin slices of Spanish onions and the seasonings, and cover over with a plate or a small dish; let it stand in a cool place for thirty minutes. Pick out the pieces of onion, dress the melon with the oil, vinegar, and lemon-juice, dust with a little paprika.

Watermelon used alone makes an excellent salad with a mayonnaise used for its dressing. It should be cut into small squares, thoroughly chilled, acidulated with a little lemon-juice, then dressed with the mayonnaise, and served on lettuce leaves or not as one prefers.

The mayonnaise dressing should be made without mustard and have a little whipped cream added to it.

Western Salad

½ pint (1 cup) sliced olives
1 gill (½ cup) diced sour pickles
½ can pimientoes
½ pint (1 cup) small cubes stale bread
Mayonnaise dressing

Mix the olives with the pickles, bread, and the pimientoes cut in small pieces. Chill, and add the mayonnaise dressing just before serving on lettuce leaves.

Yukon Salad

1 quart (4 cups) finely shaved cabbage
1 can sliced pineapple
4 ozs. (1 cup) blanched and chopped almonds
1 pint (2 cups) marsh-mallows
3 tablespoonfuls vinegar
1 quart (4 cups) whipped cream
4 ozs. (½ cup) sugar
1 tablespoonful flour
2 egg-whites
3 lemons

Cut the marshmallows in small pieces and mix them with the almonds, dried and diced pineapple, and the cabbage which has stood in ice water for one hour, then been drained and dried.

Mix the sugar and flour in a small saucepan, add the whites of eggs beaten slightly, the strained juice of the lemons, and the vinegar, and stir over the fire until it thickens. Thin and cool with the pineapple juice. Mix with the salad ingredients and fold in the whipped cream.

PICNIC FARE

THE idea of the picnic was Blondie's. Naturally, for it's the women-folk who like picnics; but the potato salad, ultra, ultra special, was definitely Dagwood's brain-storm. Things were humming in the Bumstead kitchen that bright, Summer morn.

Time marched on and presently the basket lunch was packed and Blondies chocolate cake honored with a special box of its own.

"How about this potato salad, Blondie? I want a separate container, too." Dagwood was determined to protect his masterpiece.

"All right, fill one of those large glass jars with your old potato salad. But it just makes one more package for you to carry. I'll take the cake."

Soon the Bumstead caravan moved off to the woods.

"Here's a nice place," suggested Dagwood hopefully, as they reached an open, grassy plot.

"Oh, Dagwood, look!" Blondie was eyeing a tiny island across a shallow stream. "It's beautiful, Dagwood, let's have our lunch over there."

"How could we get over that skimpy log. You might fall in."

"Dagwood!"

"Oh, okay, Blondie. I'll go over first."

Dagwood put down the basket, and tenderly the jar of potato salad, and started across the log. He made it.

"It's easy," Dagwood encouraged, "just walk out and look straight ahead. Don't forget the cake."

Blondie stepped right out.

"Blondie-e-e . . . !"

Splash!

Dagwood, wearing shoes and all, waded out to the rescue.

Back at Bumstead Manor, as Blondie came downstairs from changing, Alexander asked, "Mama, where are we going on the picnic?"

"We'll have it right here in the kitchen, darling, Daddy's in there now," replied Blondie.

He was too, contentedly stuffing in potato salad.

Blondie looked at him. And then glanced at the cake box, wet and crushed.

"My beautiful cake, it's ruined," she sighed.

"Aw, well, Blondie," Dagwood said, "it might have been my potato salad."

*   *   *

In a sense, every recipe in "Blondie's Cook Book" is adaptable to picnic fare, but on the following pages are picnic specialties, Bumstead-recommended, which will add zest to any picnic lunch. Here is a collection of recipes aimed to go on a picnic, literally, and aimed to please appetites of every kind. The Bumsteads like to go where it's permissible and safe to make a fire and do some cooking on their picnics. Hence some of their recipes call for preparation at the picnic ground. Even on a warm day a hot dish or drink gives zest to the appetite, as you know from experience.

Picnic Sandwich Fillers

Lamb Sandwiches: Roast lamb may be sliced or chopped, add some finely chopped celery, moisten with mayonnaise, and flavor with a little dried or chopped fresh mint. Spread on white or whole wheat bread.

Shrimp Sandwiches: Fresh or canned shrimps may be used. Cook in simmering salted water until pink, drain, cool and clean. Combine with an equal amount of chopped celery, moisten with mayonnaise.

Ham sandwiches: Ham may be of the home cooked or canned variety. Use it sliced if the taste of the one who is to eat it prefers, or it may be minced, seasoned with a little grated horseradish and mayonnaise, and spread on whole wheat bread for serving.

Watercress sandwiches: Spread white bread with cream or cottage cheese flavored with chopped watercress. A little cranberry or currant jelly may be added, spread on top of the cheese.

Spanish sandwiches: Chop 12 ripe olives fine with 1 small dill pickle, a bit of grated onion, into a cup of grated cheese. Use mayonnaise or other salad dressing to moisten.

Pot roast sandwiches: Use cold potroast slices with spread of chili sauce on rye bread. Or grind meat, mix with chopped pickle, moisten with mayonnaise.

Po' Boy Sandwich

This "assortment of sandwiches" can be made in dozens of different ways, depending on the tastes of the maker and what he has at hand.

The essentials are a medium-long, thin loaf of French (or Italian) bread and butter. The slim loaf is cut in two, lengthwise, buttered, and filled with an assortment that makes a whole meal. There must be at least three or four different things for filling, and they must be arranged so that each kind of filling forms a section that can be cut off as eaten.

A slice of well-seasoned tomato with crisp broiled bacon and some chopped green pepper and onion can fill one section, country sausage another, a fried or scrambled egg with chili sauce can make the next, and so on.

Adam and Eve on a Raft

Round of bread	Butter or lard
2 eggs	Salt and pepper to taste

Cut a large round of bread, and fry it in hot butter or lard until a golden brown. Then place it on a hot platter, and keep warm. Poach the eggs carefully, season and place on bread.

Grilled Liver Sausage-Burgers

Sliced raw, pan or French-fried Bermuda onion	Fat
½ inch slices liver sausage	Pickle relish or chili sauce
	Hamburger rolls

Brown slices of liver sausage slowly in fat. Turn and continue cooking until well browned. Split the buns, toast if desired, and serve the hot liver sausage slices between buttered halves. Add onion, pickle, relish or chili sauce.

Chicken Liver Spread

1 cup mashed, cooked chicken livers	2 tablespoons diced bacon
	Few drops of hot sauce
1 tablespoon lemon juice	Salt and pepper

Mix chopped chicken livers, bacon and lemon juice in a small bowl. Add tabasco or other hot sauce and salt and pepper to taste. Makes 4 sandwiches.

Potato Salad [Picnic Style]

3 lbs. potatoes	1 small onion (grated)
1 medium jar of mayonnaise	Salt

Boil potatoes in jackets. When done, peel and slice fairly thin, put into a large mixing bowl. Over each layer of potatoes sprinkle grated onion and salt to your own taste, then add the mayonnaise. Mix well. Salad should not be too moist. This is the perfect salad for picnics, Dagwood thinks.

Bedeviled Eggs

6 hard cooked eggs	½ teaspoon salt
2 tablespoons minced onion	2 tablespoons chopped, stuffed or ripe olives
2 tablespoons chopped, green pepper	Dash cayenne
	1 tablespoon mayonnaise

Cut hard cooked eggs in halves lengthwise, take out yolks and mash. Add onion, green pepper, olives, salt, cayenne and mayonnaise, pile lightly in shells, dust with paprika and garnish.

Hamburger Roll

Heat a large, soft, round roll until crisp, break open and spread with butter.

Broil a medium sized cake of chopped beef (or lamb) which has been well seasoned with salt and pepper until brown on the outside, taking care that it remains pink and juicy inside. Set in roll and sprinkle generously with chopped chives and chopped parsley. Mustard or ketchup and thinly sliced Bermuda onion add additional zest.

Broiled Deviled Hamburgers

1 lb. ground beef	2 teaspoons minced onion
4 tablespoons ketchup	1½ teaspoon Worcester-
1½ teaspoon prepared	shire sauce
mustard	1 teaspoon salt, dash of
2 teaspoons horseradish	pepper

Combine all ingredients. Split 6 hamburger rolls and toast uncut surfaces under the broiler (or over it if you're cooking on an outdoor stove). Spread cut sides with meat mixture, return to broiler and broil about 6 minutes, having meat surfaces about 3 inches from the unit.

DAGWOOD SAYS:

Fix potato salad at home but prepare the other necessities of life at the picnic spot. They'll be better—be inspired. Great outdoors have inspired great sandwiches. Take a ham, cheese, chicken, etc., and other makings along and save time spent at home making sandwiches that'll be soggy when you find a spot without a billboard in front of it.

Dill Pickles

Cucumbers
Salt
Grape leaves
Whole peppers
Dill seed
Few slices rye bread

Wash medium sized cucumbers; put a layer of salt in a pickle crock, then a layer of grape leaves, next a layer of cucumbers packed tightly. Sprinkle with salt and lay in two or three whole peppers and a sprinkling of dill seeds. Repeat until the cucumbers are used, having the top layer of dill, grape leaves and a few slices of rye bread. A few cherry leaves and grape vine tendrils will give a little variety to the flavor.

Cover with cold water, weight down with a plate and a stone, tie a paper over the crock, and leave for twelve days when pickles will be ready for use.

Egg Salad Spread

2 hard-boiled eggs, minced
2 tablespoons salad dressing
1 tablespoon chopped pickle
4 or 5 olives diced

Combine ingredients, adding a small amount of chili sauce to taste. This is something else that it's good to prepare in advance and take in a fruit jar to the picnic spot for sandwich making on the spot.

Vegetable Slaw [*Picnic Style*]

5 cups finely shredded cabbage	1 Bermuda onion
3 tomatoes cut in eighths	¼ cup French dressing
1 cucumber, sliced	½ cup mayonnaise

Combine cabbage, tomatoes and cucumber. Slice onion thin, separate each slice into rings and add to other ingredients. Mix with French dressing and mayonnaise. Serves approximately 6.

Gingerbread

⅓ cup fat	½ teaspoon soda
½ cup sugar	½ teaspoon salt
1 cup molasses	1 teaspoon ginger
1 egg	½ teaspoon cloves
3 cups sifted flour	½ teaspoon cinnamon
4 teaspoons baking powder	1 cup milk

There must be a sweet in the picnic basket, and this is easy to pack.

Cream sugar and fat together, add molasses and beaten egg. Sift dry ingredients together twice and add to first mixture alternately with milk. Bake in 2 shallow pans in moderate oven (350° F.) for 30 to 40 minutes. Serve with cream cheese or whipped cream. Use 1 cup sour instead of sweet milk if you prefer, and use 1 teaspoon soda in place of ½ teaspoon, changing the baking powder to 2 instead of 4 teaspoons.

Popovers

1 cup flour	⅓ teaspoon salt
1 cup milk	2 eggs

These are good to put in the basket for the children.

Sift together flour and salt; add eggs well beaten, also milk. Beat hard for 2 minutes, then pour at once into hissing hot, greased pans, and bake about 25 minutes in a hot oven (425° F.).

Punch Supreme

1 quart cold tea	¼ cup thick sugar syrup
1 pint grape juice	Juice 1 lemon
1 pint rhubarb juice	1 pint ginger ale

For a good, thirst-quenching picnic drink, try this. It should be carried in a vacuum jug containing a liberal number of ice cubes. But if ice cubes are unavailable, the mixture can be chilled by letting the container stand in a brook or spring.

Grape and Tea Rickey

1 quart grape juice	1 quart tea
1 quart water	1 cup orange juice
¼ cup lime or lemon juice	Sugar syrup to sweeten

Combine ingredients, sweeten to taste and serve iced. Serves 12 or 15.

Grape Cocktail Deluxe

1 cup grape juice	Sugar to taste
2 tablespoons lime or lemon juice	¼ cup charged water or ginger ale

Combine grape juice with lemon or lime and sweeten to taste. Chill thoroughly and just before serving add charged water or ginger ale.

Sweet Cherry Punch

2 cups water
1 cup sugar
2 cups canned cherry
    syrup

1 cup orange juice
½ cup lemon juice
½ cup pineapple juice
1 quart ginger ale

Make a syrup of sugar and water (corn syrup may be used for sugar), boil 5 minutes, then cool. Prepare fruit juices, strain. Add syrup and ginger ale or ice water. Should be served ice cold.

Old Fashioned Lemonade

Lemons
Fresh mint

Simple syrup
Charged water

Have a bottle of simple syrup handy for summer drinks. It mixes with cold liquids instead of settling to the bottom as grain sugar does. It's made as described in the previous recipe.

Heat lemons slightly before squeezing. This makes extracting the juice easier and gives it a smoother taste. Strain the seeds from the juice. Place a big lump of ice in a pitcher and pour the juice and charged water over the ice. Use the syrup sparingly because over-sweet drinks are not cooling. Garnish with mint sprigs. Tender young leaves of mint cooked with the simple syrup will give an extra tang to drinks sweetened with the mixture.